GREAT CARS
OF THE
FORTIES

Special thanks to the following owners for allowing us to photograph their vehicles for these pages: Dale P. Aylward (1945 Willys Jeep), Jim Baldauf (1949 Oldsmobile 88), Roy Bleeke (1948 Chrysler Town & Countrys), Marshall Burton (1949 Packard Eight), David Cammack (grey 1948 Tucker), Tony Capua (1949 Oldsmobile 98), Joseph Clampitt (1948 Dodge), Dan Darling (1940 Mercury), Al DeFabrizio (1949 Willys Jeepster), Bev Ferreria (yellow 1948 Tucker), Bob Getfried (1949 Mercury Sport Sedan), Melvin R. Hull (blue 1948 Tucker), Ralph & Carol Johnson (1948 Pontiac), Bud Juneau (1949 Buick), Jerry Malecki (green 1941 Cadillac 60 Special), Ray L. Menefee (1940 LaSalle), Burnell Mills (1941 Cadillac), Charles Newton (1949 Nash), John Otto (1941 Hudson), Arthur J. Sabin (1948 Frazer), Hannes Schachter (brown 1941 Cadillac 60 Special), Mike Scholer (1942 Willys Jeep), Jack Stuart (1940 Packard), Bob Stremmel (1941 Chevrolet coupe), Mr & Mrs. Sullivan (1941 Chevrolet convertible), Bob Ward (1949 Mercury coupe), Harry Wynn (1941 Lincoln Continental), Bob Zarnowsky (1947 Lincoln). 1947 Ford Sportsman courtesy Unique Motorcars, Rockford, Il.

Photography
Chrysler Historical Collection
Ford Motor Company Photomedia
Frank Gaines
David Gooley & Associates
Bob Hovorka
Bert E. Johnson
Bud Juneau
Vince Manocchi
Douglas J. Mitchel

Louis Weber, President
Publications International, Ltd.
3841 West Oakton Street
Skokie, Illinois 60076

Manufactured in the United States of America
10 9 8 7 6 5 4 3 2 1

ISBN: 0-517-47932-X

This edition published by:
Beekman House
Distributed by Crown Publishers, Inc.
One Park Avenue
New York, New York 10016

CONTENTS

1941 Cadillac Sixty-Special four-door sedan

1948 Frazer Manhattan four-door sedan

1941 Lincoln Continental cabriolet

1948 Tucker "48" four-door sedan

INTRODUCTION

1947 Ford Sportsman convertible

1949 Chevrolet Styleline DeLuxe wood-body wagon

1948 Pontiac Streamliner DeLuxe Eight four-door sedan

1949 Mercury coupe

1940 Packard One-Ten convertible coupe

1940 LaSalle Series 52 Special four-door sedan

The world got out of the worst economic calamity of modern times by plunging into the most devastating war in human history. World War II and its aftermath colored most every field of endeavor in many lands throughout the Forties. The American auto industry was no exception. But though this decade was rendered a short one automotively speaking—barely six years—it's left us with an unusual number of great cars. The most significant and memorable are profiled in these pages.

Detroit was already gearing up for war as the Forties opened, and its conversion to military production was almost total by the time the government ordered all civilian car manufacturing suspended for the duration in February 1942, a first for the U.S. industry. Now every automaker from American Bantam to Willys-Overland became part of the gigantic war machine that simply overwhelmed America's enemies by turning out armaments and material in unbelievable volume with unprecedented speed. The auto industry's contribution to ultimate victory was unquestionably vital, its record distinguished.

Despite this tragic interruption, the Forties witnessed startling progress in American automotive evolution. If anything, the war probably accelerated the process because it forced designers to look beyond their stillborn plans for 1943-45 once peace returned. The industry resumed production in late 1945 with warmed-over 1942 models, which sold like crazy to a public that had been unable to buy new cars for nearly four years. The result was a booming seller's market that gave most producers time to finalize their first all-new postwar designs. Except for Studebaker, which could claim to be "first by far with a postwar car" for 1947, most of these new offerings appeared for 1948-49. Not surprisingly, they make up the bulk of the cars featured here. Among them are the innovative "Step-down" Hudson and the advanced but ill-fated Tucker, both from 1948, and a raft of '49s: the most changed Ford since the Model A, the jaunty Willys Jeepster, the first of the "bathtub" Mercurys, and the Nash Airflyte, another car with styling that's earned that nickname. Here too is Buick's first "hardtop-convertible," the '49 Roadmaster Riviera, an innovation shared with GM sister divisions Cadillac and Oldsmobile, which also introduced the industry's first modern overhead-valve V-8s that season. Lincoln, Dodge, and Pontiac represent the prewar continuations of 1946-48, and the '48 Frazer Manhattan recalls the one new automaker that flourished in the postwar boom.

Of course, we haven't forgotten the prewar years. The last LaSalle of 1940, the classic '41 Lincoln Continental and Cadillac Sixty-Special, and Chevy's entire '41 line are all here. Also honored— for obvious reasons—is the wartime Jeep.

There's a lot of history in Great Cars of the Forties. We hope you enjoy it.

BUICK ROADMASTER
RIVIERA 1949

A closed coupe without the usual fixed center roof pillar wasn't exactly a new idea in 1949, and Buick wasn't alone in fielding one that season. Even so, the first Riviera helped pioneer postwar America's favorite body style, and that's why it's long been judged a great car of the Forties.

The Roadmaster Riviera shares

honors with the Cadillac Series 62 Coupe deVille and Oldsmobile's Futuramic 98 Holiday as the first modern ''hardtop-convertible.'' But contrary to popular belief, the concept did not, strictly speaking, originate at General Motors or in the years just after World War II. Dodge Brothers offered a true pillarless coupe during World War I. Introduced in 1916, it was

an all-steel three-passenger model with removable doorposts that located twin drop-down plate-glass windows on each side. Though this novel feature was aimed mainly at easier entry/exit, it also made for a car that combined the superior sturdiness and weather protection of closed coachwork with the sort of ''outdoors'' feel found in open styles. This led a number of accessory

makers to the idea of detachable "hard" tops, which became all the rage in the Twenties. Most were made of steel and covered in glossy patent leather. Many were actually stronger than even the stoutest sedan roofs of the day.

The Thirties saw increasing buyer preference for closed models with roll-up windows. This prompted development of all-steel "Turret Top" construction, which made lift-off roofs unnecessary and hastened the demise of the traditional roadster and touring car body types. Soon, engineers began finding ways to make roof pillars less obtrusive, and stylists began thinking about eliminating them altogether, especially the middle or "B" posts.

While some envisioned radical plastic "bubbletops," most designers harked back to the notion of a fixed-roof pillarless coupe with an unbroken side window area that would simulate the look of a convertible with its top up and windows down.

One of them was Buick chief stylist Ned Nickles. Sometime around 1945, he devised a 3/8-scale hardtop model and showed it to division head Harlow Curtice and Buick manufacturing manager Edward T. Ragsdale. Both liked it. Ragsdale, who ultimately worked out the design's production engineering, noted that his wife had favored convertibles for their sporty looks, but never put the tops down to avoid mussing her hair. Curtice's clout

won corporate approval for the new body style, initially as a Buick exclusive. That, of course, was later changed.

Buick chose the Riviera name to set the new hardtop apart from its other models. Billed as combining "the racy look of a convertible with the suave and solid comfort of a fine sedan," it debuted in the top-line Roadmaster series for 1949 at $3203, making it that year's second costliest offering (after the woody wagon). All Roadmasters

Besides being Buick's first hardtop, the 1949 Riviera introduced the make's soon-to-be-famous "sweepspear" bodyside moldings (owner: Bud Juneau).

7

and the mid-range Super series featured Buick's first new styling since 1942 (the low-end Special stayed with prewar lines until mid-year), though chassis design and Buick's familiar 320-cubic-inch straight eight were essentially unchanged. Appearing for the first time was a Nickles styling gimmick, the soon-to-be-famous front fender "Venti-ports," which were actually functional engine compart-

ment air exhaust outlets on early '49s. In June, another Nickles idea arrived that would also become a Buick trademark: the rakish bodyside "sweepspear" (replacing straight moldings). Dynaflow automatic, introduced as an option for the '48 Roadmaster, was extended to the Super this year, and most of the first Rivieras had it. Inside, the new hardtop boasted luxurious leather upholstery, Buick's usual flashy

dash, and a headliner decorated with convertible-style chrome ribs.

Though Buick would go on to sell hundreds of thousands of Riviera hardtops in later years, the '49 original saw just 4343 copies. Still, that was a moral victory considering Cadillac and Olds could also boast of new ohv V-8s that year and Buick couldn't. Of course, Buick would soon have a new V-8 of its own, but that's another story.

CADILLAC
SIXTY-SPECIAL 1941

T he 1941 Cadillac Sixty-Special is primarily a great car of the Thirties, the last and most visually changed version of William L. Mitchell's trend-setting 1938 original. But greatness transcends time, and this car also ranks as one the Forties' proudest achievements.

Mitchell was only 23 when his mentor, General Motors design chief Harley Earl, named him to head the Cadillac styling studio in 1936. That division had just launched its Series 60, a line of smaller V-8 models sharing the corporate B-body platform with Buick, Oldsmobile, and Cadillac's "companion" make, LaSalle. It was conceived by division general manager Nicholas

Dreystadt as a way to bolster sales by plugging the $900 price gap between the lagging LaSalle and the least costly senior cars. As the lowest-priced Cadillac since 1908, the 60 did spectacularly well, boosting division sales an astounding 254 percent and accounting for over half the make's 1936 model year volume. But Dreystadt knew that a "medium-price" image was hurting LaSalle, so he decided to bolster the new line's image by putting Earl to work on a special 60, roomier, more luxurious, and far more stylish than anything Cadillac had ever offered. Earl turned over the job to Mitchell. It was the young designer's first assignment, and his execution was brilliant.

The result appeared just two years later: a predictive four-door sedan with close-coupled styling that marked a major departure for Cadillac and made everything else on the road old-fashioned. Built on a three-inch-longer (127-inch) wheelbase, the new Sixty-Special shared the 60's basic X-member chassis design and 135-horsepower, 346-cubic-inch "Monobloc" V-8, but stood three inches lower than any previous Cadillac. Running boards were conspicuously absent, bright-work restrained in an age when

An effective facelift made the Sixty-Special seem all-new for '41, the first generation's last year (owner: Hannes Schachter).

chrome was *de rigueur*, and fulsome "pontoon" fenders accentuated the long, low silhouette. Mitchell broke new ground by eliminating the traditional belt moldings, integrating the trunk with the body, employing ultra-thin roof pillars, and framing the door windows with delicate bright bands.

With its sporty yet dignified looks, the Sixty-Special was an instant hit. It bested the entire Series 60 line by 3 to 1 in 1938 model year sales despite a 25-percent higher price and availability of just one body style. Predictably, the 1939 model saw only detail styling and mechanical changes, but two new variations appeared, a sunroof sedan and a limousine-like Imperial sedan with the sliding steel panel as well as division window. The following year brought a switch from Fisher to Fleetwood coachwork, a new Town Car model in both steel- and leather-back form, and a solid-roof Imperial. By this time, the Special's styling influence was apparent throughout the Cadillac line.

The standard Sixty-Special, which had listed at $2090 since 1938, went up to $2195 for 1941, yet it was a better bargain than ever. New rear fenders and front sheetmetal enhanced the crisply formal look and made the car appear almost all-new. Underneath were higher (7.25:1) compression, an extra 15 bhp, more torque, bigger brakes, newly optional Hydra-Matic transmission, and a more rigid frame with a one-inch-shorter wheelbase and wider front and rear tracks. Despite price competition from within a rearranged divisional lineup, the Special held to its previous annual sales of about 4000-5000 units.

The 60S became much less special for '42, simply a stretched, though beautifully finished, version of that year's massive new C-body Series 62 four-door. There was nothing wrong with that, but the change hasn't been lost on today's collectors. While a fully restored '41 now brings at least $23,000, a comparable '42 fetches less than half that, and its postwar continuations go for even less.

Though the name would live on into the Seventies, the Sixty-Speical was never quite the same after 1941. But Cadillac never forgot the magic of the timeless original, and as long as there are enthusiasts to remember, this car's great heritage will live on.

Top: The 1941 Sixty-Special previewed '42 GM styling with front fenders extended back into the door area. Above: The instrument panel was symmetrically arranged and tastefully finished (owner: Jerry Malecki). Left: Cadillac's customary "goddess" hood ornament had evolved to this highly stylized form by '41. Far left: The Sixty-Special's rear aspect emphasizes the close-coupled appearance that made this model so popular (owner: Hannes Schachter).

CADILLAC SERIES 62 1949

Cadillac made a ton of history for 1949. To its trendy, year-old "fishtail" styling the division added a modern and potent overhead-valve V-8, its first new engine in 12 years, plus a major new body style, the pillarless hardtop coupe. Though it shares credit for the last two with this year's Oldsmobile, the '49 Cadillac remains one of the decade's most influential cars. With it, the "Standard of the World" secured its position as America's most popular luxury make.

The story behind General Motors' new postwar look, first seen on the 1948 Olds 98 and all Cadillacs save the Series 75, is well known. In 1939, com-

pany design chief Harley Earl and some of his charges went to Selfridge Field near Detroit. There they got a look at the then top-secret Lockheed P-38 Lightning, a twin-engine pursuit aircraft that would be instrumental to the Allied effort in Europe during World War II. Earl was quite taken with its design, particularly the twin-boom tail, gracefully shaped rudders, pontoon-style engine nacelles, and bullet-like nose. By the time the U.S. entered the war, these and other elements had been adapted for possible use on future GM cars in a series of ⅜-scale models known as the "Interceptor" series, and this was the starting

point for 1948-49 styling. Frank Hershey, Art Ross, and division studio chief Bill Mitchell worked with Earl on the new Cadillac. Its most striking feature, of course, was the now-famous tailfins, which Earl said was used "to give the car some definition" and thus set it apart from lesser GM makes. Cadillac didn't initally refer to them as fins but simply as "rudder-type styling." It was a perfect finishing touch on a handsome overall package.

Due to production delays, the '48 Cadillacs were on the market only about nine months before it was time for the '49s. Styling was predictably unchanged apart from a lower grille

Left and below: Cadillac adopted a simpler, less costly instrument panel design for '49, dominated by a large speedometer and a winged marque crest. It replaced the drum-like 1948 affair, used only that year. Bottom: The '49 Series 62 convertible shows off its handsome lines. Styling was little changed from 1948, the first year for the divison's new postwar look, though frontal details differed slightly. The ragtop was a Series 62 exclusive (owner: Burnell Mills).

opening and wraparound chrome trim for the parking lamps. As before, the basic lineup comprised the 126-inch-wheelbase Series 61 four-door sedan and two-door fastback coupe (''sedanet''); the plusher 62, which added a convertible and, late in the season, the pioneering Coupe deVille hardtop; the four-door Sixty-Special, still on its own 133-inch chassis; and the 136-inch-wheelbase Series 75 sedans and limousines, which now acquired the new postwar styling.

But the big news was the long-awaited successor to Cadillac's durable 346-cubic-inch L-head V-8. Developed by Edward N. Cole, Harry F. Barr, and divison chief engineer Jack F. Gordon, this oversquare unit (bore and stroke: 3.81×3.63 inches) would set the pattern for all Detroit V-8s to come. It was made of cast iron, like the L-head, yet weighed 188 pounds less and produced 160 horsepower, 10 more than the old V-8 despite less capacity, initially 331 cid. Features included ample room for enlargement, wedge-shape combustion chambers, and innovative ''slipper'' pistons. The last, devised by Byron Ellis, traveled low between the crankshaft counter-weights, permitting short connecting rods and low reciprocating mass. Compression was just 7.5:1, but ratios as high as 12:1 could easily be achieved. And indeed, compression would be upped in later years as higher octane fuel become available. Displacement would go up, too.

The new V-8 made every '49 Cadillac a genuine 100-mph car. Typical 0-60 mph acceleration for the Series 62 was 13 seconds with manual shift, though some 98 percent of Cadillac buyers were specifying Hydra-Matic by this time. Nevertheless, such go was unheard-of in the luxury league, and the new V-8 even enjoyed a brief moment in the racing spotlight. A major triumph came in 1950, when Sam and Miles Collier drove a near-stock model to 10th overall at the prestigious 24 Hours of Le Mans.

With so much to offer, Cadillac racked up record 1949 model year sales, a smashing 92,554 units, eclipsing the old 1941 mark. But even that didn't stand very long, as the division went on to dominate the luxury class in the Fifties and Sixties. Today, Cadillac still reigns supreme. The '49 made it all possible.

Top: Cadillac's eggcrate grille theme was well established by '49. A slightly lower grille opening with larger eggcrates and wrapped parking light trim set the '49s apart from the '48s. Above and right: Initially referred to as ''rudder-type'' styling, Cadillac's tailfins were embryonic on the 1948-49 models, though they would grow to ghastly proportions by the end of the Fifties. Like Buick's ''portholes,'' they were used to distinguish Cadillac from other GM makes. As we know, they would be widely imitated (owner: Burnell Mills).

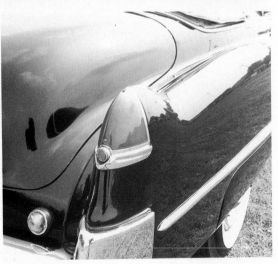

CHEVROLET 1941

The years just before World War II saw much change at Chevrolet. The new 1939 bodyshell got a major redo for 1940. Another new design arrived for '41, clearly a cousin but mostly fresh. To many, Chevy was never better than it was in 1941.

Chevy's new A-body, shared with the junior Pontiac and Olds, didn't look any larger, but passengers liked its extra interior room, shown by a three-inch stretch in front seat width. Outside, the familiar running boards seemed to be missing, but they were actually concealed by the lower door sheetmetal. Sealed-beam headlamps were new, and were integrated with the front fenders for the first time.

Riding a three-inch-longer (116-inch) wheelbase and measuring 196 inches stem to stern, the ''Fashion Plate for '41'' was a bright, perky entry in the low-price arena. Its bold, neat horizontal grille, obviously borrowed from Buick yet memorably Chevy, lured many buyers into the showrooms. And why not? The Depression seemed to be gone for good at last, aided by a national economy gearing up for an ever more likely war effort. Chevy's brisk '41 styling was the sort of thing long expected of Harley Earl's Art & Colour Studio. Compared to this year's dated, rather lumpy Ford it was sleek and refreshing yet fashionably practical.

The odds-on favorite of the younger set was the Special DeLuxe coupe, a sharp and lively car with an 80-mph top speed, 0-50 mph acceleration of about 14 seconds, and an $800 base price. Sure, the business coupe *sans* back seat cost a few dollars less, but the five-seat model was a bigger seller, with 155, 889 units. That didn't quite match the top-selling Special DeLuxe two-door Town Sedan—228,458—but it did overwhelm the four-door Sport

Chevrolet's spiffy Special DeLuxe cabriolet for '41. Production totaled 15,296 (owner: Mr. & Mrs. Sullivan).

15

Right and below: The Special DeLuxe five-seat coupe was the third most popular 1941 Chevrolet. Production was 155,889. Original list price was $800 (owner: Bob Stremmel). Bottom: Chevy's most expensive '41 was the handsome Special DeLuxe woody wagon at $995. It's a rarity now, as only 2045 were originally built. Opposite page, center and bottom: The '41 Special DeLuxe cabriolet in top-down form, and its ''art moderne'' dash (owner: Mr. & Mrs. Sullivan).

Sedan and its 59,538 units. Remaining Special DeLuxe choices were the wood-body wagon, the costliest '41 at $995 and the scarcest at just 2045 units, and the sporty cabriolet with vacuum-operated soft top, priced at $949. Buyers content with a little less trim and fewer amenities looked to the four-model Master DeLuxe line, priced from $712 to $795. All told, Chevy built over a million '41 cars, a new record. Some 60 percent were the costlier Special DeLuxe models.

But base price was just the beginning. Many owners went wild on accessories, a wide selection that was hard to resist. Fender skirts, spotlights, backup lamps, Guide rectangular foglamps, ''washboard'' front fender chrome, a grille guard and a fold-down rear guard were some of the exterior spruce-up items. Inside, the symmetrical woodgrain dash might hold a clock or one of several radios, including a five-band shortwave set. Turn signals and two-tone steering wheel (with built-in spinner) were other extras.

Mechanically, the '41 Chevy was much as before. The familiar ''Stovebolt Six'' in its reworked, 216.5-cubic-inch 1937 guise got a new cylinder head and 6.5:1 compression that boosted output to 90 horsepower, a gain of 5 bhp, and all models acquired Maurice Olley's controversial ''Knee-Action'' independent front suspension. Vacuum shift, introduced as a 1939 option, was another new standard. Gear changing required only fingertip effort as the lever traveled only a tiny distance, but shifting was sluggish and many owners eventually converted to manual transmission. A midyear addition to the line was the $877 Fleetline sedan, a forecast of 1942 and early-postwar styling. Looking like a scaled-down C-body Cadillac, it had blind rear roof quarters and a notch-back shape with a more formal air. An impressive 34,162 were sold for the model year.

Though the coupe and cabriolet have long been the most prized '41s, all these Chevys are sharp and very desirable. Some consider this to be one of the best-looking low-priced cars ever, and one of the nicest cars of any kind. This was unquestionably a vintage year for Chevrolet, and it seems almost everybody has owned a '41 at one time or other. We suspect most of those folks wish they still did.

17

CHEVROLET STYLELINE DELUXE WAGON 1949

Wood didn't seem quite so modern once America's new postwar cars arrived. True, wood had been used extensively for station wagon bodies since the early Thirties, and woody convertibles from Ford and Chrysler had drawn a lot of attention—if not many sales—in the early postwar years. But by the end of the Forties, steel was the future and wood the past, at least as far as the auto industry was concerned.

Chevy's two 1949 wagons were clear evidence of the change. The model year opened with a genuine woody,

Model 2109. Later in the year, Chevy bowed its first all-steel wagon to compete with Plymouth's new Suburban. This Model 2119 also had four doors, eight-passenger seating, even the same woody look, only the last was achieved with decals and metal trim. Both were part of the more costly Styleline Deluxe series, and the same $2267 bought either one. That was over $400 more than the Suburban, though less than Plymouth's woody. Still, no one could deny that any '49 Chevy, wagons included, was far sleeker than the squarish Plymouth—or this year's all-new Ford.

The '49 Chevrolet's main design elements had been laid down just before World War II by the General Motors Styling Staff under the direction of Harley Earl. Most notable were front fenders that flowed gently into the cowl and doors and smooth, pleasing curves throughout. A set of neat-fitting factory rear fender skirts made for nearly uninterrupted lines front to back. The two wagons were nearly identical overall. The exception was the rear quarters: straight-cut on the woody, rounded on the steel body.

Regardless of body style, the '49 was clean, modern, and far more streamlined than any previous Chevy. The curved two-piece windshield was markedly larger than the 1945-48 glass. Reduced overall body height lowered the center of gravity for improved handling, and all models looked considerably longer than suggested by

Chevrolet's last woody wagon was offered only in Styleline DeLuxe trim. Price: $2267.

All Chevys including the two wagons looked sleeker for '49 despite a one-inch wheelbase cut, thanks to the make's new postwar styling. Straight rear body quarters distinguished the woody from the very similar all-steel model introduced at mid-season, and were necessitated by the structural wood, which was less amenable to curves than metal.

their 115-inch wheelbase, which was actually an inch shorter than before. No less important to sales was construction quality, and the '49 was a standout. Unlike some of its newly designed competitors, notably Ford, this Chevy was tight and solid, with precisely fitted body panels and doors that closed with a satisfying "thunk."

As before, Chevy offered two trim levels for '49. The less costly one was now called Special, while the up-market version was the DeLuxe, with clock, lighter, and dual sunvisors included. Both were available in notch-back Styleline and fastback Fleetline models, the latter limited to two- and four-door sedans. Though popular at first, the Fleetlines lost favor and were dropped after 1952.

Under the hood of every '49 Chevy was the old reliable "Stovebolt Six," still at 216.5 cubic inches and 90 horsepower. Vacuum shift was gone, but a new manual shift linkage gave more positive action—at least until old age set in, when it tended to lock in first.

Traditionally, woody wagon bodies had been supplied by independent coachbuilders, and the '49 Chevy's was no exception. Its basic structure came from Ionia Manufacturing Company and was used for the equivalent Olds and Pontiac woodies. The latter had two taillights to Chevy's one, which was hinged to swing down with the tailgate. Exposed upper rear door hinges added to the old-timey look, as did the use of workmanlike vinyl upholstery instead of other models' standard cloth.

Compared to its earlier wagons, Chevy's last woody didn't have all that much wood in it. Most was in the tail-gate and as side trim around the windows, extending to slightly below the beltline. The midyear steel wagon used woody-look Di-Noc decals.

All-metal wagons were clearly the wave of the future, and Chevy's first steel model outsold its last woody 6006 to 3342. Of course, both those figures were only a drop in the bucket compared to the division's total 1949 model year volume of just over a million units.

The romantic woody was all but forgotten as steel wagons became enormously popular in the Fifites. Today, enthusiasts remember Chevy's last woody anew as a great car of the Forties.

CHRYSLER
TOWN & COUNTRY 1941-42/1946-48

Chrysler's elegant Town & Country appeared at the end of the prewar era, then briefly returned in the early postwar years with a somewhat different emphasis. While none of these cars were particularly exciting or even all that unique, they did have class— loads of it. Massive, opulent, impeccably finished, they remain perhaps the most desirable "woodies" ever.

Wood-body station wagons were nothing new in the early Forties, but Chrysler was the first producer to see them as something more than just humble commercial vehicles. Chrysler had never marketed a wagon under its own name. In the late Thirties, Chrysler Division general manager David A. Wallace decided it should. But instead

of the clumsy, rattling boxes then being ladled on various chassis (including Chevy, Ford, and Plymouth), he wanted a tight, streamlined wagon that looked more like a sedan. Failing to find a traditional coachbuilder who understood this concept, Wallace turned to his own engineers, who gave him exactly what he asked for.

The result debuted for 1941 as a smooth fastback-style four-door with double "clamshell" tail doors, hinged at the sides to expose an enormous cargo bay and a handsome interior with six- or nine-passenger seating. Paul Hafer of the Boyertown Body Works in Pennsylvania suggested the expressive Town & Country name. As part of the low-line Windsor series, the

new wagon rode a 121.5-inch-wheelbase chassis, with a 112-horsepower, 241.5-cubic-inch L-head six and standard Fluid Drive and "Vacumatic" transmission. Because the firm's regular body supplier, Briggs Manufacturing Company, had no experience with wood construction, Chrysler had to learn to build the T&C, and Wallace earmarked an area of the Jefferson Avenue plant for its assembly. There, a small trained workforce built the body, welded steel roof to steel cowl, and mated wood to metal with angle irons

The first Town & Country, the '41, was also Chrysler's first wagon, though it looked more like a contemporary fastback sedan (Chrysler Historical Collection).

and steel butt plates. Briggs did supply the T&C's cowl, floorpan, roof, and front sheetmetal. Everything else was Chrysler's.

With all the hand labor involved, T&C production was only 997 units for 1941. All but 200 were nine-seaters. The only changes for '42 were hidden running boards and a frontal redo, both shared with the rest of the line. Output stood at 999 when America's entry into World War II shut down all civilian car production in February 1942.

Though the T&C was the strongest wagon yet produced, Chrysler planners decided that looks and not utility was its main attraction. As the firm was already planning all-steel wagons even before the war ended, Wallace decided to ditch the T&C wagon once production resumed. In its place would be a distinct woody series with convertible, four-door sedan, formal-roof brougham sedan, two-seat roadster, and hardtop coupe. The last would have been an industry first had the firm not backed off after building just seven prototypes, essentially convertibles with welded-on coupe roofs.

Ultimately, only the convertible and sedan appeared for 1946. Like other Chryslers, these new T&Cs were mainly restyled '42s, and continued without

major change through early 1949. The former used the New Yorker's 127.5-inch-wheelbase chassis and 323.5-cid, 135-bhp straight eight. It saw 8380 copies. There were also 100 eight-cylinder sedans built, the rarest production T&C. All other four-doors were Windsor-based, with the 114-bhp, 250.6-cid six as introduced for 1942. A total of 3950 were completed.

For 1949, the T&C sedan vanished and the convertible returned with Chrysler's first new postwar styling, a four-inch-longer wheelbase, and mostly

carryover mechanicals. Just 1000 were built. The T&C's last hurrah was 1950, when the sole entry was a wood-trimmed New Yorker-based version of the belated Newport hardtop. Production stopped at 700. After this, the name was applied only to wagons.

Lately, the T&C idea has been revived for the compact, front-drive LeBaron convertible. Nice car, but plastic wood and robot welders just don't compare with real planking and hand craftsmanship. Just ask anyone who's ever owned the genuine article.

Above and opposite page, top: Two pristine 1948 Town & Country convertibles. Like other early postwar Chrysler cars, the T&Cs saw only detail changes. The original mahogany wood inserts were replaced by Di-Noc decals in 1947, though they looked much like the real thing (owner Roy Bleeke). Opposite page, bottom: The 1946 convertible with "white doughnuts." Below: The 1941 wagon (Chrysler Historical Collection).

DODGE
CUSTOM
1946-48

Dependability may be dull, but it does have rewards. Take Dodge, for instance. Since its founding in 1914, the make had prospered with sturdy, no-nonsense transportation, and becoming a division of Chrysler Corporation in 1928 did nothing to change that. Dependability remained almost synonymous with Dodge in the years right after World War II, and that's precisely why we rank its early postwar models as great cars of the Forties. They're significant as representatives of the product philosophy that had enabled Chrysler to overhaul Ford Motor Company as the nation's second largest automaker in that worst of economic times, the Thirties.

Chrysler had built its early high success primarily on engineering, and with few exceptions its cars had always been mechanically superb but aesthetically drab. There was a reason for this: beginning with Walter P. Chrysler himself, the company had always been run by engineers, who tended to be conservative in their approach to design, if not disinterested. Then too, the firm's one attempt at progressive styling, the Chrysler and DeSoto Airflow of the mid-Thirties, had been a bust, and the experience made management even more reluctant to try anything even remotely radical. Reflecting this attitude was K.T. Keller, who took over as company president on Walter Chrysler's death in 1940. Himself an engineer, Keller was not without a sense of style, but he cared far more about practical points like passenger room and driver visibility. Naturally, his engineer-stylists gave him what he wanted, with the result that, as one wag put it, Keller's cars

1946-48 Dodge styling was typical of the early-postwar period. Dash was new and more glittery. This '48 bears the more detailed 1947-48 ram mascot (owner: Joseph Clampitt).

mildly restyled continuations for 1946-48. Dodge, like its corporate siblings, retained its basic prewar styling, which had been laid down with the 1940 models by former company designer Raymond H. Dietrich, the famed Thirties coachbuilder. The Dodge facelift, based partly on wartime studies, was handled by A.B. ''Buzz'' Grisinger, John Chika, and Herb Weissinger. Allowed bolt-on modifications only, they did a remarkably effective job. The main change was a chromier, cross-hatch grille. Inside was a gaudier new dash that retained full engine instrumentation but departed from prewar practice in its asymmetrical layout.

Mechanically, the first postwar Dodge was much like the last prewar model. Wheelbase remained at 119.5 inches, with a 137.5-inch chassis reserved for a low-volume seven-seat sedan. Power was still supplied by a 230.2-cubic-inch L-head six, which was inexplicably rated at 102 horsepower, 3 bhp less than before. Mechanical changes included moving the starter from a foot pedal to a button on the dash, twin-cylinder front brakes, standard inline fuel filter and full-flow oil filter. Fluid Drive returned as an option and became standard for 1947-48, an important sales plus. Dodge retained its then-customary two-tier model lineup, with base DeLuxe and fancier Custom trim levels spanning six body styles. Initially, prices ranged from $1229 for the DeLuxe business coupe to $1743 for the long-chassis Custom sedan. By the end of this series in early 1949, the spread had moved up to $1587–$2179.

After a slow start, Dodge finished 1946 in fourth place behind Chevy, Ford, and Plymouth, contributing mightily to Chrysler's fortunes in the booming seller's market. Volume improved for 1947, but the make slipped to fifth. It then rebounded to fourth for 1948. Aside from a bit more detail in the traditional ram hood ornament for 1947-48, the basic design was absolutely unaltered until Chrysler's first new postwar models arrived in early 1949.

Time has a way of changing perspective, and the 1946-48 Dodge doesn't seem nearly so dowdy now as it did when new. Maybe that's because time also tends to develop character in both people and cars. This Dodge certainly has character. We should all age so well.

Top: Roomy interiors with chair-height seats characterized all Chrysler products designed in the reign of president K. T. Keller. Above: Central stoplight was a feature of all early-postwar Chrysler cars. Elongated rear deck marked club coupes. This Dodge Custom cost $1774 for '48 (owner: Joseph Clampitt).

''wouldn't knock your eyes out, but they wouldn't knock your hat off, either.''

Once car production resumed in late 1945, Chrysler followed most of Detroit by hauling out its 1942 dies and issuing

FORD SPORTSMAN 1946-48

T he singular 1946-48 Ford Sportsman is memorable not so much as a car as for its mission. Simply put, it was designed to lure buyers back to the showrooms after World War II by adding a touch of glamour to a very familiar-looking model line.

As the war drew to a close, most U.S. automakers had to decide between getting back into volume production quickly with warmed-over prewar products or putting the rush on all-new postwar designs. Except for Studebaker, everyone did the former. Ford Motor Company had no choice. Though financed to the tune of $700 million, it was heavily in debt and now faced the huge cost of winding down

its war effort. Moreover, the death of company president Edsel Ford in 1943 and a resulting series of key personnel departures had left one of the nation's largest employers in disarray, beset by power struggles among the old guard that remained.

It was for this reason that Edsel's son, Henry Ford II, was given early discharge from the Navy, and he returned to Dearborn in September 1945 to take the helm of his family's ailing company. "HF II" knew that there wasn't enough time or money for getting out brand-new designs until 1948 at the earliest. And, as it turned out, there was really no need: a car-starved public was more than happy to buy

almost anything on wheels, even recycled '42s. But he still wanted to offer something different, reasoning that if the first postwar Fords couldn't be all-new, at least some of them could be strikingly different on the surface. Paneling convertibles in maple or yellow birch with mahogany-veneer inserts seemed like a pretty good way to do that.

The handsome wood-body Ford Sportsman saw 2250 copies for '47. Another 28 were sold as '48s (owner: Unique Motorcars).

The result was the Ford Sportsman and a kissin' cousin, the Mercury Sportsman, the first product decisions made by the new man in charge. The concept had originated during the war with former styling director E.T. "Bob" Gregorie. It attracted HF II because it was easy and cheap to execute. The company already had a massive timber forest and processing plant at Iron Mountain, Michigan that had been supplying raw materials for Ford's woody wagons since 1936, and a convertible would be no more costly or difficult to build.

Each Sportsman began as a stock convertible with a section of rear sheetmetal cut away, replaced by a steel "skeleton." To this was fitted the wood framing, which was fully struc-

tural, made from solid wood blocks and mitred together with handcrafted precision. All 1946 Ford Sportsmans used "A" type framing with full-length horizontal members. Later cars employed "B" and "C" styles with vertical segments. The 1946 rear fenders didn't match the wooden trunklid's new curvature, but 1941 sedan delivery fenders did.

Otherwise, the Sportsman was much like any other 1946-48 Ford. It was offered only in upper-level Super DeLuxe trim and only with the 100-horsepower, 239.4-cubic-inch flathead V-8, essentially the existing Mercury unit now adopted for all V-8 Fords, and not the 90-bhp ohv six. Standard equipment included hydraulic window lifts, leather

28

Besides its unique wood body construction, the Sportsman differed from other 1946-48 Fords in using rear fenders from the 1941 sedan delivery and having standard leather upholstery and hydraulic window lifts. Offered only in top-line Super DeLuxe trim with the familiar flathead V-8, it was fielded mainly as a showroom traffic builder (owner: Unique Motorcars).

upholstery, and dual visor vanity mirrors, all of which lifted initial base price to $1260, some $500 above the standard ragtop.

Despite its high price and only scant promotion, the Sportsman was a fair success. The first one was delivered to film actress Ella Raines on Christmas Day 1945, just three months after Henry Ford II took over as company president. Another 1208 followed for '46. The '47 saw 2250 copies, plus another 28 that were reserialed as 1948 models. (The Mercury version appeared only for '46. Just 205 were built.) Weighing 100 pounds more than the standard convertible, the Sportsman wasn't super-quick, but it could hit 85 mph flat out and 60 mph from rest in just under 20 seconds.

The Sportsman would be Ford's only non-wagon woody, but it wasn't the only one on the postwar market. Nash had its novel Suburban sedan, Chrysler its beautiful Town & Countrys. Still, the Sportsman accomplished its mission. Today, it's a Ford to remember and cherish, a handsome reminder of a unique period in American automotive history.

FORD 1949

Model year 1949 brought the most dramatically changed Ford since the Model A had replaced the Model T a generation earlier. But that's not why we remember this as a great car of the Forties. The '49 literally saved Ford Motor Company from extinction. Had

it not succeeded, it's doubtful the firm would have survived the Fifties.

Ousted in the Thirties by Chrysler Corporation as the nation's number-two automaker, Ford Motor Company had emerged from World War II with decidedly cloudy prospects. Old-hat

design, steadily declining sales, and turmoil in the executive suite had left the company reeling, with losses as high as $10 million a month in 1946-47. Such conditions were intolerable for a firm so vital to the nation's economy, and they prompted the early discharge

from service of Henry Ford II, grandson of the company's legendary founder. "HF II" acted quickly, bringing order to chaotic business practices, hiring a bright young group of managers called the "Whiz Kids" from Litton Industries, and coaxing Ernest R. Breech from the Bendix Division of General Motors. He also got his designers cracking on new postwar products, including Harold Youngren, a Breech recruit from Oldsmobile, and styling consultant George W. Walker.

A fully revamped corporate lineup with seven different platforms was in place by early 1947. Scheduled debut was 1949, the year that would see a brand-new Chrysler fleet and completion of GM's postwar overhaul. But Breech had doubts, and he convinced Ford's policy committee to cut the number of basic building blocks to four. The casualties: a compact Ford, a new-generation Continental, and the proposed standard Ford. The last would be fully redesigned.

What emerged was a Ford completely new in every way except wheelbase, still 114 inches, and engines, still the familiar 239.4-cubic-inch flathead V-8 and 226-cid ohv six. The changes started with a modern ladder-type frame, replacing the previous, heavy X-member affair for all models save the convertible. Ford's antiquated twin-

Opposite page: The 1949 Ford Custom V-8 convertible, $1886. Above: The $1511 Custom V-8 club coupe (Ford Motor Co. Photomedia).

31

transverse-leaf-spring suspension was junked for independent front suspension via wishbones and coil springs and a live rear axle on longitudinal semi-elliptic leaf springs. Torque-tube drive gave way to Hotchkiss, the transmission was fully reengineered, and the old two-speed rear axle moved aside for modern, optional overdrive. This chassis supported a shorter, lower, wider new body with contemporary flush-fender styling. Though often credited to Walker, the design was actually the work of Richard Caleal, with assistance from Bob Bourke and Holden Koto, two his former colleagues on the Raymond Loewy team at Studebaker. This accounts for the ''bullet'' grilles worn by both the '49 Ford and the 1950-51 Studebaker. Careful attention to detail brought curb weight down by over 500 pounds to under 3000 for all but convertible and woody wagon, which made the '49 Ford livelier than its predecessors despite the carryover engines.

The '49 Ford bowed in June 1948 because the company literally couldn't afford to wait for the usual fall introduction. This only accelerated the crash development program, which cost $72 million, pretty high for a firm just recovering from a lot of lean years. Workmanship and quietness both suf-

fered as a result, but the '49 Ford was a solid hit and lifted Dearborn to a much-needed profit of $177 million for the calendar year. Model year production was better than 1.1 million, which bested Chevy by over 100,000 units. Calendar year output was the best since 1929.

As in 1946-48, Ford retained a two-series model line for '49. The six-cylinder Standard comprised business and club coupes and Tudor and Fordor sedans. To these the V-8 Custom group added a convertible and a structural-wood wagon with two doors instead of

four. With prices ranging from $1333 to $2119, this lineup had something for just about everybody. With it, Ford's future was assured.

Today, the '49 Ford and its more refined 1950-51 continuation remain significant cars with a wide collector following. What else would you expect from a piece of modern history?

Below: Ford's '49 Custom V-8 Fordor sedan. Price: $1559. Bottom: The $2119 Custom V-8 wagon (Ford Motor Company Photomedia).

FRAZER MANHATTAN 1948

The Frazer was the product of an uneasy alliance between a 35-year auto industry veteran and a brash industrialist who thought it might be nice to get into the car business. The veteran was master salesman Joseph W. Frazer. The industrialist was west coast steel and shipbuilding tycoon Henry J. Kaiser.

Frazer had learned his trade in the Twenties at Packard, Pierce-Arrow, and General Motors. He moved on to help build Chrysler Corporation, then breathed new life into Willys-Overland in the Thirties. Shortly before the U.S. entered World War II, Frazer and his associates had acquired the remnants of Graham-Paige Motors with the idea of producing a new postwar car. Frazer was looking for a moneyed partner in early 1945 when friends introduced him to Kaiser, whose pockets were bulging from fat wartime contracts. The two hit it off, and Kaiser-Frazer Corporation was born. Together, they acquired the mile-and-a-half-long ex-bomber factory at Willow Run, Michigan, and Henry laid plans to build there his hoped-for full-size Kaiser, with unit construction, torsion-bar suspension, and front-wheel drive.

In base form, the Frazer Manhattan four-door sedan sold new for $2746. K-F built 18,591 in all (owner: Arthur J. Sabin).

33

Graham-Paige in Detroit would see to the costlier Frazer, a rear-drive companion sharing the Kaiser's basic body design, the work of famed stylist Howard A. "Dutch" Darrin.

Problems loomed early. The front-drive Kaiser "85" proved unworkable, and finances forced G-P to sell its automotive interests to K-F in early 1947. Yet despite these woes and postwar materials shortages, K-F managed to start production by June 1946. The Frazer remained a costlier Kaiser, which was now reengineered with rear drive and a separate box-section chassis with conventional suspension and a 123.5-inch wheelbase. Both makes were built at Willow Run, initially at a ratio of one Frazer to every two Kaisers.

K-F prospered in the booming postwar seller's market. Its cars had the industry's first true flush-fender

styling, offered an unheard-of array of colors and trims, rode well, and were solidly built. Only one body style, a four-door sedan, was offered in each line through 1948, Kaiser Special and Custom, Frazer standard and Manhattan. Power came from an improved, automotive version of the Continental "Red Seal" industrial engine, a markedly undersquare 226.2-cubic-inch six rated at 100-110 horsepower.

By New Year's Day 1950, what some obsevers called the "postwar wonder company" had built some 400,000 cars under both marques. But by then the bubble had burst. The pivotal year was 1949, when Henry tried to maintain 1948 production levels in the face of brand-new Big Three competition and only minimal styling changes in his own products. High prices didn't help. A Kaiser Special cost more than a Chrysler Windsor, and the Frazer sold

for as much as some Cadillacs, which now had a potent new V-8 and much sleeker looks. The result was a considerable drop in sales that left K-F with thousands of unsold cars. Leftovers were accordingly given 1950 serial numbers just to clear stocks. This debacle and continuing friction with Henry and his son Edgar prompted Joe Frazer's resignation as company president in 1949. Edgar moved in to replace him. K-F's downhill slide to oblivion had begun.

The Frazer's last year was 1951. Left-over Kaiser utility sedans, with double rear hatch and folding back seat, were converted into Frazer Vagabonds, and the previous Kaiser Virginian pillared hardtop became a Frazer Manhattan. All models were treated to reshaped sheetmetal, but prices were higher than ever and production stopped at a little more than 10,000 units. Altogether,

about 152,000 Frazers were built for 1947-51.

Ironically, the Frazer disappeared even as dealers were clamoring for more of the cars. It was typical of the mistakes that led to the demise in the U.S. of K-F itself after 1955. Manage-ment briefly considered a new Frazer based on the lovely second-generation Kaiser, introduced for 1951, but with Joe Frazer out of the picture it was not to be. With the marque died America's first postwar convertible sedan and a potential that was never fully exploited.

Opposite page and above: It seems rather dumpy now, but the Frazer was quite trendy for its day, thanks to the industry-leading flush-fender styling. Above left: Joe Frazer's family coat of arms served as the car's crest. Above left: 226-cid six was no ball of fire. Top: Dash has typical period layout (owner: Arthur J. Sabin).

HUDSON 1948

Low-slung, ground-hugging, roomy. Such words were used to hype many of Detroit's first all-new postwar cars, but the "Step-down" 1948 Hudson was one of the few that truly deserved them. It was unquestionably one of the decade's most outstanding designs.

Hudson broke a lot of new ground with its '48. Since 1932, the firm had touted "unit engineering," a body bolted to its chassis instead of resting on flexible mounts. With the Step-down it switched to a more solid welded structure as pioneeered in the Thirties by the Chrysler Airflow and Lin-

coln Zephyr, and Hudson took the concept a step further by dropping the floorpan so that it was fully surrounded by the chassis siderails. This put the floor lower than the door sills, hence the "Step-down" nickname, while affording girder-like side-impact protection.

Besides safety, the Step-down's chassis design contributed to a much lower center of gravity that made this one of the best-handling cars on the road. It also contributed to the styling, which looked like something out of "Buck Rogers" next to the 1946-47 Hudsons. The basic slab-sided torpedo shape originated in "aerodynamic" quarter-scale models created in 1942-43 by a team made up of Bob Andrews, Dick Caleal, Holden "Bob" Koto, and Strother McMinn, led by Art Kibiger and chief company stylist Frank

Spring. Early ads insisted that the '48 put buyers "face to face with tomorrow." Fortunately for Hudson, the new look was a success with both dealers and the public. A generous 124-inch wheelbase and 207.5-inch overall length enhanced the low, sleek lines of all the new Step-downs, as did an overall height of barely 60 inches, almost nine inches less than 1946-47 and two inches lower than Raymond Loewy's new postwar Studebakers. Overall width bulged by more than four inches to over 77, which added to

the interior spaciousness of the Step-down's "Monobilt" structure.

Violating the old Detroit rule about restyling and reengineering in the same year, Hudson brought out a new "Super Six" for '48. At 262 cubic inches and 121 horsepower, this under-square L-head unit (bore and stroke: 3.56 × 4.38 inches) was the industry's

The 1949 Hudsons were virtually identical with the '48s. Here, the '49 Commodore Six sedan. Price was $2383 (owner: John Otto).

Top: Hudson's long, low 1948-49 torpedo styling was distinctive for its day. Above: The "Step-down" sedan's roomy cabin. Interior details of the rare factory air conditioning (above) and the more popular radio (owner: John Otto).

largest and most powerful six. By 1951 it would evolve into the 308-cid Hornet powerplant, the largest modern L-head six ever and king of stock-car racing in 1952-54. Hudson's prewar 128-bhp, 254-cid straight eight returned unchanged from 1946-47. Buyers could choose from four transmissions: the standard three-speed manual, manual with overdrive ($101), "Vacumotive Drive" ($47), and "Drive-Master" ($112). Vacumotive engaged and disengaged the clutch via the gas pedal. Drive-Master added semi-automatic operation. With the lever in High, it shifted between second and third gears whenever the gas pedal was released.

Offered in Super Six and Eight and Commodore Six and Eight series, the '48 Hudsons were about 13 percent heavier (3460-3800 pounds) model for model than their immediate predecessors, which aided roadability, Prices were heftier too, and rose several times during the model year. Nevertheless, Hudson had a good season, producing 117,200 cars, nearly two-thirds with sixes. The convertible brougham with its unusually wide windshield header was a late arrival. Offered only in Super Six and Commodore Eight form, it saw just 1177 copies. Today they're the most sought-after of the early Step-downs.

Except for serial numbers, the '49 Hudsons were identical with the '48s. Production rose to 159,100 units for the model year, lifting the make from 10th to 9th place. It was as high as Hudson would ever get. Innovative though it was, the Step-down, like all unitized cars, was more difficult and costly to change than a conventional body-on-frame design, and sales were never high enough to pay for anything more than modest annual styling changes. Hudson did manage a hardtop coupe beginning in 1951, but it lacked funds to build a hoped-for station wagon, which probably would have sold well, or a V-8. Steadily dwindling sales led to the 1954 merger with Nash that formed American Motors. The make was then killed off just three years later. Thus, the Step-down stands as the last "real" Hudson.

LASALLE 1940

LaSalle was the most romantic and longest-lived of the several General Motors "companion" makes that appeared in the late Twenties. The 1940 models were the last of the line, and they were arguably the best. In retrospect, Cadillac was correct to drop its "junior edition" when it did. But it's a tribute to this marque's enduring aura of class, style, and distinction that the division has occasionally flirted with the idea of a new LaSalle over the past 45 years—as recently as the early Seventies, in fact.

Along with Buick's Marquette, Oakland's Pontiac, and Oldsmobile's Viking, the LaSalle was born out of GM president Alfred Sloan's desire to offer "a car for every price and pocketbook." Its mission was to fill the price gap Sloan had detected between Buick and Cadillac, and it amply

accomplished that in its early years. Introduced in 1927, it accounted for fully 25 percent of total division sales and by 1929 it was outselling Cadillac 11 to 9. LaSalle immediately established itself as a style leader thanks to the efforts of young Harley Earl, whom Sloan had hired specifically for this project. It was the 1927 model that launched him on an illustrious 30-year career as Detroit's dean of design.

Throughout the Thirties, LaSalle provided the sales volume that helped Cadillac survive in the decimated Depression market. Though total division output rarely exceeded Packard's, LaSalle's share was often substantial and sometimes crucial. But GM managers wanted much more, so LaSalle was transformed from a less expensive luxury product into an upper-medium-price entry for 1934,

with less distinguished coachwork and an Oldsmobile L-head straight eight in place of the previous Cadillac-built V-8. The formula changed again for 1937, as LaSalle adopted the 322-cubic-inch V-8 from the 1936 Cadillac Series 60 while continuing with the corporate B-body, by then boasting all-steel "Turret Top" construction. Production set a new record, only to fall by half the next year due to the 1938 recession. Sales again proved disappointing for 1939, which brought all-new styling, more glass area, a shorter wheelbase, an optional metal sunroof for sedans, and slightly lower prices.

The last 1940 model was arguably the best-styled LaSalle of all. Shown: The Series 52 Special sedan (owner: Ray Menefee).

The problem was obvious. By 1940 the LaSalle had been all but squeezed out of its once well-defined market niche by the costlier Buicks and the lesser Cadillacs, both of which it had come to resemble closely. An improving national economy and Cadillac's decision to concentrate solely on the luxury field also hastened the junior make's demise.

But LaSalle was never better than it was in 1940. The V-8 tacked on five horsepower for a total of 130, and interiors were more spacious thanks to a three-inch wheelbase stretch (to 123 inches). The smooth, clean styling was marked by sealed-beam headlamps artfully integrated into the front fenders and striking "catwalk" openings either side of the LaSalle grille, which had always been narrower and more delicate than Cadillac's. There were now two distinct series for the first time. The plusher 52 Special offered four-door sedan, two-door coupe, and convertible coupe and sedan. The base Series 50 added a two-door sedan to these styles. Prices ranged from $1240 for the Series 50 coupe to $1895 for the 52 Special four-door convertible, of which only 75 were produced. LaSalle contributed 24,130 units to Cadillac's overall 1940 volume of about 37,000, but that wasn't enough to prolong its life. Though the division went as far as a full-scale mockup for a '41 LaSalle, the make was superseded by the new low-price Cadillac Series 61, which sold well, largely by dint of its more prestigious nameplate.

LaSalle lasted only 15 years, but it's never been forgotten by old hands at GM. In 1955, Harley Earl's studio created two design exercises for that year's Motorama, a two-seat roadster and a hardtop sedan, both called "LaSalle II." The name cropped up

again on early proposals for what became the 1963 Buick Riviera, then a decade later as a suggestion for the compact 1976 Seville sedan. Cadillac may yet revive LaSalle. Until then, we can rejoice in the glorious '40.

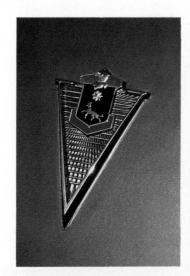 

An all-around look at the 1940 LaSalle Series 52 Special sedan. Instrument panel was recognizeably Cadillac, but on a smaller scale. The division's fondness for heraldry showed up on the trunklid crest and on the inner door panels. This model originally sold at $1440 (owner: Ray Menefee).

LINCOLN CONTINENTAL 1941

The words "Edsel" and "styling" rarely appear together without prompting memories of the car that proved a disaster for Ford Motor Company back in the Fifties. But "Edsel," as in Edsel Ford, Henry's only son and company president in the Thirties, was responsible for one of the most revered automotive designs of all time: the matchless 1940-41 Lincoln Continental.

From the moment it appeared, it turned heads and made even normally conservative types eager to part with lots of cash just to own one. Today, nearly a half-century later, it still does.

Edsel had dreamed of making Lincoln the best car in the world ever since his father had acquired Henry Martyn Leland's second automaking enterprise (Cadillac was the first) in 1922. Though always in the shadow of his great father and thus something of a tragic figure, Edsel was blessed with an unerring sense of style. It was readily apparent in the masterful K-series Lincolns of the Thirties as well as more ordinary cars like the Ford Model A and 1932 V-8.

It was in the Thirties that Edsel became enamored of certain European cars, especially their narrow, upright grilles, long hoods and front fenders, and other elements he thought of as "continental." Believing such themes could be successfully applied to an American car, he collaborated with E.T. "Bob" Gregorie, the young head of Ford's design department, on a special convertible body for the production Lincoln Zephyr chassis. Completed in late 1938, the car was sent to Palm Beach, Florida, where Edsel used it during his annual winter vacation. It immediately attracted over 250 inquires as to when it might be offered for sale. Encouraged by this response, he okayed a production version as an addition to the 1940 Zephyr line, and his personal car reached Lincoln showrooms with only the barest of changes from the original design.

The result was one of the first Forties cars recognized as a true classic. Officially a Zephyr, the Continental appeared without any identifying name script as Edsel's four-seat cabriolet and as a closed coupe. Naturally, its 125-inch-wheelbase chassis and 292-cubic-inch, 120-horsepower V-12 were shared with Lincoln's junior series, but masterful long-hood/short-deck proportions made the Continental longer overall than equivalent Zephyrs. It was also heavier, thanks to the considerable leading involved in the mostly hand-built body, so it didn't handle quite as well. Even so, the Continental was agile for a car of its day weighing nearly two tons, not to mention being highly refined and handsomely furnished. Only the finest broadcloth and leather were used for the upholstery, and the radio speaker, horn ring, control knobs, and instrument bezels were covered in genuine gold plate. With all this, the Continental was hardly cheap—$2916 for the cabriolet, $2783 for the club coupe—and this plus the painstaking craftsmanship explains why production was only 54 and 350 units, respectively, for the model year.

The Continental became a separate series for 1941 and saw higher production, 400 cabriolets and 850 coupes. Changes were few. Appropriate name script, combined turn signal/parking lamps, and pushbutton door releases were the main distinguishing points outside. Alterations were more substantial—and less welcome—for '42. A flashy facelift that prefigured immediate postwar styling brought higher, squared-up fenders and added seven inches to overall length, so weight went up. A larger 305-cid V-12, used only this year, provided an extra 10 bhp. Production for the war-shortened season was just 336 units combined.

During and immediately after the war, a number of proposals surfaced for a new Continental, including a wood-body derivative of the new-generation Lincoln scheduled for 1949. In the end, all came to naught. The 1942 Continental returned for 1946 with the original 292 engine and largely carry-over styling. It vanished after 1948.

Today, the 1940-41 "Mark I" remains the most revered Continental, which is as it should be. After all, there's nothing like an original.

Top: The Continental cabriolet's price was reduced for '41 to $2865 (owner: Harry Wynn). Above: The companion club coupe sold that year for $2812, a $29 increase.

LINCOLN 1946-48

Some great cars have died with their names. Others have lived on in name only. The breakthrough Lincoln Zephyr lived on after its name. To be sure, the last "official" Zephyr, the 1942 model, did return after World War II, but the modified 1946-48 version was simply called "Lincoln." Now why would Ford Motor Company's prestige make want to forget the name of the most successful product in its history, the one that had literally saved it from the ravages of the Depression? Please read on.

Introduced for 1936, the Zephyr was to Lincoln what LaSalle was to Cadillac and the One-Twenty to Packard: a medium-price "junior edition" intended for higher sales volume in the face of greatly reduced luxury-car demand brought on by "hard times." The basic design was inspired by a radical rear-engine prototype devised by the forward-thinking John Tjaarda, with pioneering unit body/chassis construction that was retained on the production Zephyr, though with a conventional front-engine/rear-drive layout. The

Zephyr also boasted streamlined styling, mainly the work of chief company stylist E.T. "Bob" Gregorie, and was far more attractive than that other early streamliner, the slow-selling Chrysler/DeSoto Airflow, which had arrived a little over a year before. Finally, the Zephyr could claim the

The ex-Zephyr Lincoln sedan was virtually unchanged from 1946 to '47. The '47 is shown (owner: Bob Zarnowsky).

only V-12 in the medium-price field. Developed along the lines of the Ford flathead V-8 by chief engineer Frank Johnson, this 267-cubic-inch engine featured aluminum-alloy heads, a cast-iron block with the cylinder banks angled at 75 degrees, and four main bearings. It packed 110 horsepower.

With all this, the Zephyr generated sales figures previously unheard of at Lincoln, swelling the make's 1936 model year output by 10 times its paltry 1935 level. It might have done even better had it not been for that V-12, which had problems from the start. The main ones were inadequate crankcase ventilation that caused sludge buildup, and too-small water passages that led to overheating, bore warpage, and ring wear. To some degree, these maladies were dealt with the first year. Yet despite the adoption of hydraulic lifters for 1938 and cast-iron heads and oiling improvements for 1942, this engine never shed its trouble-prone image. And that's one reason why the Zephyr

name failed to return after the war. Ironically, the V-12 had been made much more reliable by that time.

Zephyr production more than doubled for 1937, when a three-passenger coupe and a plush Town Sedan joined the existing two- and four-door sedans. Revised front sheet-metal and a three-inch-longer (125-inch) wheelbase marked the '38 line, which added a convertible coupe and sedan. Sales declined due to a national recession, then recovered to near 21,000 for 1939, when the big change was Ford's long-overdue hydraulic brakes. The 1940 models looked much the same but were, in fact, structurally all-new. The V-12 was bored out to 292 cid and 120 bhp, the convertible sedan vanished, a five-seat coupe-sedan replaced the three-passenger coupe, and richer interiors were offered. Production inched upward, but the Zephyr was now overshadowed by the dashing new Continental.

After detail updates for '41, the Zephyr was restyled for '42. Higher,

squarer fenders added weight and length, and the general look was more glittery than before. The V-12 was bored to its maximum 305 cid, good for 130 bhp, and a hastily contrived automatic, called "Liquimatic," arrived as a reply to Cadillac's Hydra-Matic.

The wartime production hiatus and the end of Cadillac's LaSalle after 1940 also figured in Lincoln's decision to drop the Zephyr name on the '42's postwar continuation. The 1946-48 redo saw a gaudy die-cast grille with Cadillac-style eggcrate, a return to the 1941 engine size, five fewer horsepower, plus fewer body styles and no more long-wheelbase Custom offerings. Despite these mostly retrograde changes, the no-name Zephyrs sold fairly well, with about 42,500 built for the period.

The postwar Zephyr would be the last 12-cylinder car in U.S. series production. That plus interesting period styling accounts for the new-found interest in these cars among enthusiasts. It's long overdue.

The Zephyr's "no-name" postwar continuation retained basic 1942 styling, but grille was new and some
minor trim changed in detail. Rear doors continued to
be hinged at the back, "suicide" style, and opened to
reveal a spacious, flat-floor interior with plush chair-
high seats, all very much the norm for the early to
mid-Forties. A custom interior option, a reminder of
Lincoln's once-vast array of coachbuilt models, added
$168 to the $2554 base price of the 1947 four-door
sedan. It was also available for the club coupe but not
the convertible, the only other body styles offered in
these years. Lincoln's V-12 returned to its 292-cid,
1941 size for 1946-48. It put out 120 bhp (owner: Bob
Zarnowksy).

MERCURY 1940

Ford Motor Company bolstered its place in the medium-price field with introduction of the Mercury for 1939. Mainly the idea of Henry Ford's only son Edsel, then company president, the new make was conceived as a "super deluxe" Ford to fill the big price gap that had long existed between Ford and the Lincoln Zephyr. Initially, it was carefully priced somewhat below Oldsmobile and about even with the Pontiac Eight. Though Mercury wouldn't match the volume of these GM rivals in its early years, it did average about 80,000

annual sales through most of the Forties, good for 12th or 13th place in the industry production standings. This represented important new business for Dearborn, and it couldn't have come at a better time.

Mercury's arrival coincided with a low point in Ford Motor Company's fortunes, which wouldn't begin to improve for another decade. Though Ford had long been able to boast the industry's only low-price V-8 cars, as well as the innovative Zephyr and the great coachbuilt K-series Lincolns, old Henry's hidebound adherence to out-

moded engineering like mechanical brakes and leaf-spring, solid-axle front suspension had cost the company dearly in the high-volume market. Mercury was part of Edsel's plan to reverse the steady sales slide, and it was shrewdly planned to keep development costs low and thus help the firm conserve cash.

The first-year Mercurys looked much like the 1939 Fords, which was a plus. E.T. "Bob" Gregorie, the company's young chief stylist, gave both makes one of the most pleasing shapes of the late prewar era. The

major design elements were a crisply pointed prow bisecting a vee'd grille, headlamps moved into the front fenders, and rounded overall lines characteristic of "first-generation" streamlining. The Mercury arrived on a four-inch-longer (116-inch) wheelbase and was somewhat heavier than the Ford. To compensate for the extra weight, Edsel specified a bored-out version of the familiar Ford flathead V-8, with 239 cubic inches and 95 horsepower instead of 221 cid and 85 bhp. Body styles were limited to four five-passenger types: two-door sedan and coupe-sedan, four-door

Mercury entered its second year with only minor changes from the 1939 debut edition and maintained close mechanical and styling similarity with Ford. Sealed-beam headlamps were common to both makes—and the industry in general—for 1940, but a longer chassis gave Mercury more interior space and its larger flathead V-8 provided more power for superior go. Four-door Town Sedan was one of five 1940 body styles (owner: Dan Darling).

Town Sedan, and two-door convertible. Prices ranged from $916 for the two-door sedan to $1018 for the convertible. An important new mechanical feature shared with other Ford Motor Company products this year was Henry's long-shunned hydraulic brakes.

The handsome Town Sedan on these pages is from the follow-up 1940 line. The basic 1939 design was little changed apart from adoption of sealed-beam headlamps, in line with the rest of the industry, and a minor but effective facelift in the manner of the ever-popular '40 Fords. A new offering was a smart convertible sedan, but this body style was waning in popularity, so it disappeared after this one year and about 1000 copies. Mercury sales as a whole were brisk, however, with production reaching a little more than 81,000 units, a gain of some 6000 from the make's inaugural year. Part of this was no doubt due to a growing reputation for performance equal to its name. Despite its extra weight, a well-tuned stock Mercury was quicker than a Ford V-8 and was usually capable of turning close to 100 mph. This ''hot car'' image would remain with Mercury well into the Sixties.

Mercury and Ford both added extra pounds and inches for 1941, becoming somewhat bulkier-looking in the process. Model year 1942 brought even blockier sheetmetal and more chrome, the look that would return for 1946-48 pending release of Ford Motor Company's first all-new postwar designs for 1949.

While the 1930-40 Fords became collectible automobiles long ago, the equivalent Mercurys have only now begun to attract a significant following. In a way this is odd, because the Mercs have the same winning style and the basic honesty of flathead V-8 power that give the Fords their timeless appeal. Perhaps Mercury's usual role as a ''super deluxe'' Ford had something to do with it. Then again, that's no bad thing to be.

Above: The 1940 Mercury dash was a bit nicer than Ford's (owner: Dan Darling).

MERCURY 1949

Mercury marked its 10th birthday by becoming a "junior Lincoln" for 1949 instead of a "senior Ford." Enthusiasts have been celebrating ever since. Though Dearborn's medium-price make would again switch identities several times in later years, none of those transformations would be more successful than this one. With styling that still pleases today, plus fine performance and a little help from Hollywood, the first of the "bathtub Mercs" remains not only a great car of the Forties but one of the most popular models ever to bear the name.

The 1949 Mercury would have been a somewhat different kettle of fish had it not been for a last-minute change of plans. Ford Motor Company had tar-

geted 1949 as the year for a wholesale shift to its first new postwar designs, which had originated in wartime studies that were carried out as time permitted. These were finalized once peace returned, and by early 1947 no fewer than seven different platforms were envisioned. At the bottom was a 100-inch-wheelbase "light car" compact, followed by a standard Ford on a 118-inch chassis and a brace of Mercurys on wheelbases of 120 and 123 inches. At the top of the corporate heap was a trio of Lincolns: a 125-inch-wheelbase standard series, a 128-inch-wheelbase Custom/Cosmopolitan line, and a 132-inch-wheelbase Continental and limousine. It was a logical progression that would have given Ford much

broader market coverage against General Motors than it had ever had. But it didn't exactly suit Ernest R. Breech, fresh from GM and Bendix as second-in-command to recently installed company president Henry Ford II. At Breech's insistence, the proposed Ford was hastily redesigned on a 114-inch wheelbase, the Continental was axed as unprofitable, and the compact was shipped off to Ford France as unnecessary in the postwar U.S. market. Mercury was then assigned to the 118-inch platform, the standard Lincoln

The road-hugging coupe was the second most popular '49 Mercury, with 120,616 built. It cost $1979 new (owner: Bob Ward).

moved to a 121-inch chassis, and the 125-inch size was adopted for the top-line Lincoln Cosmopolitan.

All of Ford's 1949 models were well-received, but none more than Mercury. The familial resemblance with Lincoln was a plus for most buyers, as was the styling itself: clean, massive and sleek. Though wheelbase was unchanged, the '49 looked longer than the '48, and it was much lower. The same four body styles returned—coupe, wagon, convertible, and four-door sedan. The last, now called Sport Sedan, retained "suicide" style rear-hinged back doors. The wagon switched from four portals to two, though it retained partial wood construction. Prices ranged from $1979 to $2716, making Mercury good value in that year's market.

Besides new looks, the '49 boasted Mercury's first independent front suspension (via coil springs) and a more powerful flathead V-8, stroked from 3.75 to 4.00 inches (on the same 3.19-inch bore) for 255.4 cubic inches and 110 horsepower. Merc-O-Matic shelf-shift transmission was still two years away, but there was a $97 "automatic overdrive" option that brought a shorter 4.27:1 final drive, which improved off-the-line go compared to the normal 3.90:1.

With its slightly sinister styling, the '49 Mercury—and the basically similar 1950-51 models—quickly became a favorite among America's car-crazy youth, who applied special grilles, lowered and sectioned bodies, and added cruiser skirts and other accessories. The use of a tail-draggin' customized Merc in the James Dean film *Rebel Without a Cause* only hastened the elevation of this design to "cult car" status. Of course, Ford was more concerned with sales than status, and the '49 Mercury was a solid smash. Production more than tripled from the make's previous best model year total, topping 300,000 units, and Mercury skyrocketed from 16th to 6th on the industry volume list in just one year.

Mercury's basic '49 design lasted through 1951. But enthusiasts tend to flock to the first of any breed, especially if it's a great one. The '49 Merc was certainly that. No wonder it's still so vividly remembered.

Center spread and right: The '49 Mercury coupe and its flashy dash (owner: Bob Ward). Far right: The two-door woody wagon.

NASH 600 1941

Unit construction wasn't a new idea in 1941, but it was unheard of in the low-price field. Nash wanted a bigger share of that market, and its all-new unibody 600 series managed that formidable task rather well.

The 600 arrived to replace the LaFayette, which had seen dwindling sales since its status had changed from separate ''companion'' make to the bottom-of-the-line Nash series for 1937. *Time* magazine called the 600 ''the only completely new car in 1941.'' As the first high-volume model

with a modern welded unit structure, it was. It was also the most popular unit car to date, and gave Nash a powerful shot in the sales arm.

Stylish yet tough, the 600 was engineered mainly for economy. The model designation derived from its purported 30-mpg fuel economy, which meant 600 miles between fill-ups of its 20-gallon tank. Such frugality was indeed possible under ideal highway cruising conditions, though Interstates were still decades into the future. Initial ads were more modest—

and honest—in claiming ''over 500 miles to the tankful.'' To reinforce the economy theme, Nash dubbed the 600's engine ''Flying Scot.'' This was a brand-new L-head six with the typically undersquare bore/stroke dimensions of the day (3.13 × 3.75 inches) and a not-so-typical feature, manifolds cast into the block. On lowly 6.7:1 compression, it produced 75 horsepower from its 172.6 cubic inches. With its ''frame and body welded into one twist-proof, rattle-proof unit,'' as the ads boasted, the 600 was com-

paratively light for its size, weighing in about 400-500 pounds under an equivalent body-on-frame model. Performance was thus adequate, though hardly startling.

Visually, the 600 was much like its big brothers, the Ambassador Six and Eight. Proportions were scaled down to a 112-inch wheelbase, nine inches shorter than the senior models', and overall length measured 194 inches. Nash continued with its Ford-like

The new 600 looked much like Nash's 1941 Ambassador Six and Eight, but its shorter platform made it lighter and thriftier. Shown is the $837 DeLuxe fastback four-door sedan, one of the eight models available. Nash claimed 30-mpg fuel ecomomy for every one.

front prow for '41. This year's ensemble had the nose surmounting a full-width lower grille composed of thin horizontal bars, with two upper segments on either side looking for all the world like electric shaver heads. Though it was shorter between wheel centers, the 600 shared the same newly designed bodyshell adopted across the board this year, so there was plenty of room inside for six adults, who sat in chair-height comfort on seats nearly five feet wide. Also enhancing ride were ''gentle'' coil springs all-round, another first for the low-price class.

The 600 was not only the first unibody car in the low-price field but one of the least expensive cars in its class. Model offerings comprised business coupe and two- and four-door sedans in base Special trim, with pricier DeLuxe versions of these styles along with two ''trunkback'' sedans. The Special four-door fastback went for $805, less than a comparable Ford V-8 DeLuxe, while the Special business coupe cost a mere $730. DeLuxe prices ranged from $772 to $880. Convertibles, alas, were offered only to Ambassador buyers.

Available 600 options included overdrive, then known as ''automatic cruising gear'' or ''fourth speed forward,'' and two-tone paint with ''harmonizing'' interiors. Also on the list were the pioneering ''Weather Eye'' heating/ventilation system, a Nash innovation since 1938, and a rear seat that could be converted into a makeshift travel bed in a claimed 60 seconds.

Nash had a good 1941 sales year, and the 600 was a big part of it. Model year output was 84,007 units, a gain of some 18,000 from 1940. Of the estimated 80,000 units for calendar '41, well over half were 600s. Nash had the good sense to leave well enough alone for '42, though the 600 came in for the same major front-end restyle applied to its costlier linemates. Production fell to only 31,780 units in this abbreviated model year. The same basic cars would be back after World War II for a three-year reprise.

The 600 helped a lot of people on the home front get through the war. After all, 25 mpg meant a lot when ''A'' ration coupons limited purchases to four gallons or less a week. The miserly 600 engine would continue in various guises well into the Sixties.

Top: Sharply pointed fronts were a styling feature of several makes in the late Thirties and early Forties, and Nash was one of them. Like the senior Ambassadors for '41, the 600 ensemble consisted of a Ford-like prow with upper and lower grilles. Above: A peek inside the 600 DeLuxe fastback four-door sedan reveals an instrument panel with the ''post-Art Deco'' adornments typical of the period. Note the add-on turn signal stalk.

NASH AIRFLYTE 1949

Unforgettable is one way to describe the 1949 Nash Airflyte. Ugly is another. Beautiful? Some folks certainly think so, but they're a minority. The "bathtub" Nash had its share of detractors when it first appeared, and it still evokes "love-it-or-hate-it" responses today. Yet in its day, many thought this car worthy enough to buy one, enough to put Nash back in 10th place on the industry production chart.

Though several late-Forties designs earned the "bathtub" nickname, the Airflyte probably deserved it most. The styling was functional, however. In fact, this was about as aerodynamic as a postwar car ever got. The basic shape is claimed with some authority by Holden "Bob" Koto, who collaborated with Ted Pietsch in 1943 on a scale model that looked much like the eventual production design. In an age when wind tunnels were almost unheard of, the Airflyte boasted a total air drag of only 113 pounds at 60 mph, versus up to 171 pounds for contemporary Packards. The result—then as now—was improved highway fuel economy. Besides the "inverted airfoil" body, "airflow management" was aided by wheels skirted at the front as well as the rear, which unhappily made for a much wider-than-normal turning circle and cumbersome tire changes.

Beneath its futuristic exterior, the Airflyte boasted a number of advanced features, some old, some new. Per Nash tradition, it employed unit con-struction, with body and frame "built as a single, rigid, welded unit—squeak-free and rattleproof," according to the ads. All instruments were housed in a "Uniscope" pod atop the steering column, easy to see but not so easy to repair. Seats were high, comfy, and quite wide, and convertible front seats allowed the interior to serve as an emergency motel, much to the chagrin of parents with teenagers.

Mechanically, the Airflyte was a carry-over. The base 600 series stayed with a

Nash's all-new 1949 Airflyte Ambassador Custom four-door sedan sold new for $2363 (owner: Charles Newton).

57

172.6-cubic-inch L-head six rated at 82 horsepower, while the senior Ambassador continued with its 234.8-cid, 112-bhp straight eight. Respective wheelbases were 112 and 121 inches. Overall height was 62 inches for all models. Body styles were limited to two- and four-door sedans and a two-door Brougham sedan. Low-line Super, mid-range Super Special, and top-shelf Custom trim levels were available for each, with prices ranging from $1786 to $2000 for 600s to $2170 to $2363 for Ambassadors. Besides lowering body drag, the Airflyte's long wheelbases and resulting overall length provided a gentle, rolling ride, aided by low-rate, long-travel coil springs at each wheel.

Though it had finished as high as seventh in 1932, Nash usually ranked 11-13th in industry model year output. The Airflyte helped the independent automaker to record volume for '49 with 135,238 units. That was just ahead of Studebaker and right behind ninth-place Hudson, its future partner in American Motors.

For 1950, the Airflyte adopted a larger backlight for improved outward vision, and the 600 name was retired in favor of Statesman for the junior series. The 172.6-cid six went into Nash's new compact, the pioneering Rambler, so a long-stroke 184-cid version substituted in the Statesman. Seat belts and "airliner" reclining front seatbacks

were newly available, as was automatic transmission. The latter arrived in the form of Hydra-Matic, borrowed from General Motors but fitted with "Selectro-Lift Starting" (instead of turning a key you pulled up on the gearlever to fire the engine). Volume improved, but Nash slipped back to 11th. It regained 10th on still higher production for 1951, when the main styling change was more prominent rear fenders. By this time the public had tired of "bathtubs," but Nash was ready with an all-new 1952 design, completed with more than a little help from the great Italian coachbuilder, Pinin Farina, and bearing a more modern "three-box" shape.

Automakers wouldn't again show much interest in aerodynamics until the late Seventies. While it's doubtful that any Detroit designer ever looked to the Airflyte for inspiration, its influence is evident in low-drag show cars like the Ford Probe IV. So if function is beauty, then maybe the Airflyte wasn't so ugly after all.

Opposite page: The Ambassador's 112-bhp, 234.8-cid straight eight and Nash's infamous travel bed. Above: The '94 Airflyte's "uniscope" instrument pod (owner: Charles Newton).

59

OLDSMOBILE 1949

Oldsmobile wasn't first with a modern postwar V-8, but it did set the pattern for the next two decades of Detroit performance. The year was 1949. The engine was the legendary Rocket.

Cadillac had been working on a successor to its long-running L-head V-8 since the Thirties. The Olds V-8 didn't get going until 1946. It was a completely independent effort, largely the work of Gilbert Burrell, assisted by Elliott M. "Pete" Estes (who became General Motors president in

1974). Nevertheless, both new power-plants were ready for the start of 1949 production and were quite similar in design, with overhead valves, wide bores, short strokes, "slipper" pistons, and short, stiff crankshafts. This was no surprise, as both followed principles laid down by Charles F. Kettering, the "grand old man" of GM Engineering. Harold Metzel, then an Olds engineer and later division general manager, recalled that "Olds interest in a new engine was motivated by the thought that performance and fuel economy

needed improvement. We were impressed [by] Kettering's experiments with a [high-compression] engine. We looked more to research lab results than we ever did to Cadillac."

Initially designated "8-90" and "Kettering," the new Olds engine bowed as the Rocket V-8, a name very much in line with the aircraft and spaceship imagery then favored by Detroit's marketing moguls. Like the Cadillac unit, it ran on fairly low compression, 7.25:1, but was designed for up to 12:1 without major tooling

changes, anticipating the availability of higher-octane postwar fuels. Initial capacity was 303.7 cubic inches on bore and stroke of 3.75 × 3.44 inches. Output was 135 horsepower at 3600 rpm. On learning of the Rocket, Cadillac raised displacement of its own V-8 from 309 to 331 cid, which yielded 160 bhp at 3800 rpm.

Though well-established as GM's "innovator" division, Olds was quite cautious in introducing radical new developments. Thus, the Rocket V-8 was originally slated only for the senior 98 series, where it duly ap-

Olds offered its 98 four-door sedan only in Deluxe form for '49. New Rocket V-8 was now standard (owner: Tony Capua).

The A-body, Rocket-engine 88 arrived in early 1949. Offered only in base trim, the convertible sold at $2559. Just 5434 were built (owner: Jim Baldauf).

peared at the start of the 1949 model year. It worked wonders for the top-line models' performance compared to their previous 115-bhp straight eight, but Metzel knew the Rocket would really show its stuff in the lighter, Chevy-size Olds 76, which was still trundling around with a 100-bhp L-head six. He and chief engineer Jack Wolfram easily persuaded Olds general manager Sherrod E. Skinner to lobby corporate brass for approval to combine the two. It was a timely idea, since the junior Olds had just come in for "Futuramic" styling, the division's term for GM's new postwar look created by company design dean Harley Earl. Skinner carried the day and the 88 was born, arriving some three months behind the rest of the line in February 1949. Like the 76, it shared the new-look A-body with this year's Chevrolet and Pontiac, but rode a completely different suspension, with four-wheel coil springs and lever shocks, anti-roll bars at each end, and two massive stabilizer bars to help locate the live rear axle. In fastback club coupe form the 88 weighed some 300 pounds less than a 98 sedan, making this par-

ticular model ideal for the newly emerging sport of stock-car racing. Seven rear axle ratios were offered but only one transmission, Oldsmobile's pioneering Hydra-Matic automatic.

Despite its abbreviated debut selling season, the 88 accounted for almost a third of Oldmobile's record 1949 production, which soared by some 116,000 units to 288,310. The little-changed 1950 version did even better, which prompted Olds to drop its six-cylinder cars the following year. We should also not forget a new 98 entry for '49,

the lovely Holiday. Along with this year's Buick Roadmaster Riviera and the Cadillac Series 62 Coupe deVille, it was the industry's first volume hard-top. An enormous success in later years, it was added to the 88 series for 1950 in two versions.

In just two short years the 88 would be eclipsed by the Super 88 as the Olds image leader. Still, the '49 original stands as the granddaddy of all Detroit's "hot ones" in the Fifties and Sixties, and that makes it a car worth honoring.

PACKARD ONE-TEN 1940

The Packard One-Ten has never been treated kindly, even by the marque's most ardent loyalists. Long snubbed as unworthy of the Packard name, it's often been blamed for starting the make's long, slow slide toward oblivion in the Fifties. But it ain't necessarily so.

One-Ten was the new 1940 name for the Packard Six. Arriving for 1937 as a short-wheelbase derivative of the eight-cylinder One-Twenty, it completed the firm's remarkable transformation from a low-volume builder of virtually hand-made luxury cars to a much larger and more modern concern with sales in the industry's top 10.

That metamorphosis had begun just two years earlier with the One-Twenty. The first Packard specifically designed to be built in high numbers, it was conceived by sales wizard Max Gilman and former General Motors production specialist George T. Christopher, both of whom had been recruited by company president Alvan Macauley to devise a more profitable medium-price product than the firm's first such effort, the 1932 Light Eight. Like its predecessor, the One-Twenty was intended to keep the company alive in the face of a luxury market that had dwindled by that time to a scant two percent of total new-car

sales. Also like the Light Eight, it was a genuine Packard, with the make's typically conservative styling, fine workmanship, and a smooth, robust engine. But careful attention to production economics enabled the One-Twenty to sell for only about half as much and still make money, which the Light Eight never did.

Aimed at all those people who had

Now called One-Ten, Packard's six-cylinder 1940 convertible coupe listed at $1104. Only the wagon cost more (owner: Jack Stuart).

always coveted a Packard but had never been able to afford one, the One-Twenty sold like nickel hamburgers. Packard soared from 17th to 12th in the model year production race, then moved up to ninth. Bolstered by the new Six, the make set an all-time production record for 1937 and claimed a solid eighth in the industry rankings.

The One-Twenty was renamed Eight for 1938 and was totally reworked along with the Six. Wheelbases grew by seven inches for both, to 127 on the former and to 122 on the latter, and Packard's traditional ''ox-yoke'' radiator announced a more rounded body of the ''second-generation'' streamlining school. Horsepower ratings were unchanged, but the 120-horsepower, 282-cubic-inch straight eight got a number of detail improvements and the 237-cid L-head six was bored out to 3.50 inches, good for 100 bhp and 246 cid on the 4.25-inch stroke shared with the eight. Two- and four-door touring sedans, business and club coupes, and convertible coupe were offered in each line, plus a convertible sedan and DeLuxe four-door for the Eight. The latter was also available with three Rollston custom styles on a 139-inch chassis and as a seven-seat sedan and limousine on a 148-inch wheelbase. Despite these improvements, Packard volume fell by over half, mainly due to the 1938 recession.

Both junior Packards were largely the same for 1939, but the One-Twenty name returned and a woody wagon was added to each series. New features included the aptly named ''Handishift'' remote-control gearlever and ''Econo-Drive,'' the firm's first commercially available overdrive. As it had since introducton, the Six continued to outsell the One-Twenty.

The Six was renamed One-Ten for 1940, and both juniors acquired ''catwalk'' auxiliary front grilles in a minor facelift. Detail technical changes included another round of suspension tweaks and newly optional all-electric Warner Gear overdrive. The One-Ten legnthened its sales lead over the One-Twenty to better than 2 to 1, a margin it held through 1941. That year brought the handsome new Clipper, which spelled the end of the junior

lines' traditional Packard styling. For 1942, the Clipper look was applied to all One-Ten/One-Twenty body styles save the two-door convertible.

In most years, the junior Packards accounted for more than three-fourths of the make's total production. Without them, the company couldn't have survived the Thirties. For this reason alone, the last of the prewar breed stand as great cars of the Forties. ''Ask the man who owns one.''

PACKARD EIGHT 1949

Packard's first all-new postwar generation merits "great car" status not only for its prestigious nameplate but as the last Packard to sell in really high numbers. Despite ungainly "pregnant elephant" styling, the 1948-49 models brought

Packard production to a new peak: 208,499 units in all. Sadly, the make would never do as well again.

Strictly speaking, these Packards were not "all-new." Oh, there were two new engines and an expanded lineup with an extra wheelbase choice,

but their basic body and chassis engineering built heavily on the 1946-47 continuation of the prewar Clipper. Introduced for 1941, the Clipper was designed by the eminent Howard A. "Dutch" Darrin and modified for production by Packard

styling chief Werner Gubitz. Its flowing fenders, hidden running boards, tapered tail, and smooth overall contours signalled Packard's shift away from traditional square-rigged styling, and the new look was so well received that it was applied to almost all of the firm's 1942 models.

Beautiful though it was, the Clipper somehow seemed quite dated when it returned after the war, but Packard was hard at work on an extensive facelift. This was inspired by the final version of the Phantom, a one-off landau-roof convertible coupe created in 1941 for company stylist Ed Macauley, but the results in 1948 production form were debatable. Management dictated filling out the Clipper's bodysides with sheetmetal to give the effect of flow-through fenders, but it only added some 200 needless pounds and made the car look unfortunately fat, hence the ''pregnant elephant'' sobriquet. A short, squat grille hardly helped.

If styling wasn't its forte, the '48 was still very much a Packard for refinement, comfort, ride, and craftsmanship. Sixes were absent from the model lineup for the first time since 1937. The new order began with Standard, DeLuxe, and Super Eight offer-

Lack of mid-bodyside moldings makes this '49 Super Eight convertible a ''first series'' model. Base price was $3250. Packard built only 1237 (owner: Marshall Burton).

ings on a carryover 120-inch wheelbase, with a 141-inch chassis reserved for seven-passenger Super sedans and limousines. The Super engine was a new 327-cubic-inch L-head unit with markedly undersquare dimensions (bore × stroke: 3.50 × 4.25 inches), five main bearings, and a rated 145 horsepower. The lesser Eights used a "squarer" (3.50 × 3.75), 288-cid powerplant with 130 bhp. At the top of the line was the Custom Eight, distinguished by an eggcrate grille (other models used simple horizontal bars) and powered by Packard's existing—and excellent—356-cid straight eight with 160 bhp, five less than before. Custom offerings comprised convertible and two fastback sedans on a 127-inch wheelbase and the expected seven-passenger sedan and limo on the customary 148-inch-wheelbase platform. The seven-seaters were

rather sad reminders of the halcyon custom-body days at Packard in the Thirties and early Forties. However, there was a novel new body style for '48, the Station Sedan. Offered only in the Standard Eight series, it was the first Packard wagon since 1941 and one of Detroit's last woody wagons. In common with others of its day but unlike its predecessors, the Station Sedan relied on wood for structural support mainly around the tailgate. Real tree bark did appear around the windows and on the doors, but it was purely decorative.

The '48 Packards continued into 1949 completely unchanged except for a nominal 5-bhp increase for the two smallest engines. A "second series" lineup appeared in May of that year, distinguished mainly by an extra chrome molding along the body. A new Super DeLuxe Eight sub-series

arrived with the Custom's eggcrate grille, and the long-chassis Customs were dropped. Packard marked its 50th anniversary with Ultramatic, the only automatic fielded by an independent producer without help from a transmission manufacturer. Combining a torque converter with multiple-disc and direct-drive clutches, Ultramatic was smoother than GM's Hydra-Matic, but it provided only leisurely acceleration and was less reliable.

The "pregnant elephant" lasted through 1950. Today, it's appreciated anew as Packard's last real success and a great car of the Forties.

The first-series 1949 Packard Super Eight convertible. Styling was termed "pregnant elephant" for obvious reasons (owner: Marshall Burton).

PONTIAC 1946-48

In late 1945, American automakers started picking up where they'd left off before World War II. Pontiac was no exception. Introduction of brand-new postwar designs was some three years away for most companies, due to materials shortages and lack of time. General Motors was further hampered by a major strike that erupted in November.

But it didn't matter. For the moment, getting back to civilian production was the industry's top priority. The reason was pent-up demand. The public had gone nearly four years without new cars, and most buyers were happy to pay full list price or more for anything on wheels—even warmed-over '42s—as long as it was new. The result was an unprecedented seller's market.

Pontiac weighed in with a car that many remembered as being pretty

nice in prewar form. Like its GM sisters, the division had acquired newly designed bodyshells for 1940. These got a minor facelift for '41 and a more extensive restyle for '42. That year's main design innovation was Harley Earl's "pontoon" front fenders swept back into the door area for the first time. Predictably, this basic look was little changed on the 1946 continuation, which started coming off the lines in October 1945. Appearance alterations, devised by Robert J. Lauer, involved a more horizontal look for the full-width grille, parking lamps moved behind it, and elimination of the upper bodyside moldings. The by-now traditional "Silver Streak" hood trim and Chief Pontiac mascot continued. Because of shortages, only the B-body Streamliner two-door fastback was initially available. The full line wasn't in place until June 1946.

As before, Pontiac's first postwar offerings were grouped into Torpedo and Streamliner series, the former with "trunkback" styling on the corporate A-body platform. Respective wheelbases were 119 and 122 inches; overall lengths were 204.5 and 210 inches. Each was available with a choice of two carryover engines, a 239.2-cubic-inch L-head inline six with 90 horsepower or a 248.9-cid straight eight with 103 bhp. The eight cost about $30 extra. Also returning unchanged was the ladder-type 1942 chassis, with independent front suspension and a leaf-spring/live-axle rear end featuring wood liners to limit interleaf friction. Options also stayed pretty much the same. Among them were rear fender skirts, a choice of three radios, and

Pontiac's 1948 Streamliner DeLuxe Eight sedan (owners: Ralph & Carol Johnson).

white plastic wheel trim discs in lieu of the hard-to-get whitewall tires. Also available were high-compression heads for both engines and a choice of rear axle ratios, a 3.90:1 "economy" setup or a 4.55:1 "mountain" gearset.

Like its prewar predecessor, the '46 Pontiac was softly sprung and easy to handle. Gearshifting was almost effortless thanks to the standard vacuum-assist linkage, and a strong first gear helped initial acceleration. Both engines offered impressive low-rpm torque that let the driver "lug down" in third and then pull smoothly away without downshifting.

Everybody did well in the booming postwar seller's market, and Pontiac was no exception here, either. Its output of 137,640 units for the model year was good for sixth place in the 1946 standings. Pontiac held this position for '47 despite a mostly unchanged group of cars that saw nearly double the sales volume. For 1948, the division carried out what was effectively a model realignment by offering most of its cars with a deluxe trim package as a $90-$120 option. It included chrome fender moldings, gravel guards, and

Chief Pontiac's streamlined countenance continued to grace 1948 hoods. Dash was simple if quite shiny. This model's original price was $1814 (owners: Ralph & Carol Johnson).

wheel discs. More significant was first-time availability of GM's Hydra-Matic automatic transmission at $185. It was especially welcome by eight-cylinder customers, who now far outnumbered six-cylinder buyers. Largely on the strength of this, Pontiac set a new production record of 235,000 units and moved up to fifth, where it

would remain through 1953.

Though Pontiacs would become a lot more exciting in a few years, these early postwar models were mainly solid, reliable family cars that, per long-standing tradition, were a step up from Chevrolet. That may not make them great cars of the Forties, but it doesn't hurt, either.

TUCKER 1948

Though not nearly so controversial anymore, the predictive, short-lived Tucker "48" remains one of the most fascinating chapters in automotive history. In a sense, it's a great car of the Forties that never really was.

The story begins with Preston Thomas Tucker, one-time assembly line worker, sales executive, and police officer, who had helped the famed Harry Miller built front-drive Indianapolis racers in the Thirties. Optimistically inclined but often unpredictable in temper, Tucker had dreams of building his own automobile, and what he had in mind was truly different. By the time World War II was underway, he envisioned a radically styled two-door fastback with a Miller-designed, air-cooled flat six mounted at the rear, plus all-

independent torsion-bar suspension, disc brakes at each wheel, a windshield that would pop out harmlessly on impact, and doors cut up into the roof. The really way-out items were classic cycle-type freestanding front fenders and a central "cyclops eye" auxiliary headlight, both of which would turn with the front wheels. Miller died in 1943, so Tucker asked Ben Parsons to finalize the engine for production. In December 1945, Tucker announced that his "car of the future"

would go on sale in 1948. The race was on.

Taking advantage of the government's willingness to back new postwar ventures, Tucker agreed to float a $15 million stock issue to lease the 500-acre Chicago complex where Dodge had built B-29 bomber engines during the war. Next he was approached by free-thinking stylist Alex Tremulis, who translated his original concept into a producible car in only five days. A running prototype,

dubbed "Tin Goose," was ready by spring 1947, but its Miller engine was soon deemed impractical. Tucker found a ready-made substitute at Air-cooled Motors in Syracuse, New York, a water-cooled version of the 335-cubic-inch flat six from the wartime Bell helicopter, rated at 166 horsepower.

The Tucker "48" was distinctive coming or going. This is #22 of the 50 production cars built (owner: David Cammack).

Unusual ''cyclops eye'' front marks all Tuckers. Below left and right: Car #41 (owner: Bev Ferreira). Bottom: Tucker #19, with non-period slim-band whitwalls (owner: Melvin R. Hull).

What emerged from all this was a full-size four-door fastback with startling looks and performance to match. Built on a 128-inch wheelbase, the production Tucker stood just 60 inches high, measured 219 inches long, spread 79 inches wide, and weighed 4200 pounds. The missile-like overall shape suggested the ''Torpedo'' name breifly used in ads, and Tremulis estimated its drag coefficient at 0.30, excellent even now. Drum brakes and more conventional suspension components were substituted to hold down costs. A dropped floorpan, a benefit of the rear-engine layout, lowered the center of gravity, and combined with unusually wide tracks for exceptional handling. It also made for a very spacious interior. Preston's insistance on occupant safety brought recessed driver controls and a novel

''Safety Chamber,'' promoted as a refuge for front seat occupants ''to drop into, in a split second, in case of impending collision.'' Retained were the planned ''cyclops eye'' and pop-out windshield. With the best power-to-weight ratio of any U.S. car to date, the Tucker was capable of 0-60 mph in 10 seconds and at least 120 mph flat out.

With all its advanced features, the Tucker caused quite a stir. It probably would have sold well, but it never had a chance. The War Assets Administration blocked company bids on two key steel-making facilities, and Preston alienated several of his own associates, some of whom started rumors to undermine him. His take-over of the Chicago plant raised eyebrows at the Securities and Exchange Commission, which launched

a fraud investigation in June 1948 amid a rising tide of bad publicity. The Tucker factory was forced to close that August after building just 37 cars. Another 13 were later hand-built by volunteers from leftover parts. Then, a confidential SEC report was deliberately leaked to the press in early 1949 by commissioner Harry McDonald, a political appointee of Michigan senator Homer Ferguson. As Tucker said later, it ''marked the beginning of the end.'' After a four-month trial, he was acquitted of all charges in January 1950, but by then his dreams had evaporated.

Tucker insisted that his car was ''too good,'' a victim of the Detroit establishment. History as proved him correct. Ironically, he was working on yet another car when he died in late 1956.

WILLYS ARMY JEEP 1942-45

Is any vehicle better known than the military Jeep? Not likely, unless it's the Ford Model T or Volkswagen Beetle. Not surprisingly, they're similar in several ways. All were known for rugged construction, no-frills simplicity, and all-purpose dependability. And in the minds of their owners—or uniformed drivers—all had near-human personalities. These were more than just vehicles: they were friends.

The Jeep served beyond the call of duty during World War II on eastern and western front alike. Whether at Anzio or along the Burma Road, from South Pacific jungles to the shifting sands of North Africa, the Jeep was sure to be there, doing whatever was required—and more. It was conceived mainly for reconnaissance, but its service record was far more varied. Jeeps carried troops, both well and wounded, mounted guns, hauled

supplies, guarded lines, delivered messages, and transported everyone from commanding generals and VIPs to rank-and-file GIs. Even President Roosevelt used one when reviewing the troops. Army chief of staff General George Marshall called it

The Jeep MB had evolved to this familiar, blunt-nose look by the end of World War II. Gun is a dummy (owner: Dale A. Aylward).

"America's greatest contribution to modern warfare." Few who knew it disagreed.

Credit for the Jeep concept goes to American Bantam, the pioneering compact-car maker of 1936-41, which also developed the initial prototype and participated in wartime production. But the name is forever tied to Willys-Overland, which submitted a competing proposal and turned out the military version in huge numbers in 1941-45. Willys made only the chassis, however. Bodies came from outside suppliers.

Willys' first Jeep was the "Quad" prototype, delivered to Camp Holabird, Maryland, on Novevember 11, 1940. Finalized under company engineering vice-president Delmar G. "Barney" Roos, it was, per Army specifications, a lightweight, quarter-ton utility vehicle with four-wheel drive, and had a curved, snout-like front. After extensive testing, the basic design was accepted, and full-scale development began at the Willys plant in Toledo. The "Quad" was followed by a second prototype in

1941, the MA, created to counter alternatives from Bantam and Ford. Wearing a flat, vertical-bar grille and headlamps perched atop the front fenders, it rode an 80-inch wheelbase and measured 130 inches long. Power was supplied by the 134.2-cubic-inch L-head four from the 1941-42 Americar passenger models, churning out 63 horsepower. Willys built exactly 1577 of the MAs. Some time later, it turned

to the eventual military version, designated MB. It was identical with the MA except for being two inches longer, weighing 2450 pounds, and having a fold-down windshield and headlights built into the front grille area. There were no doors, of course. By war's end, Willys had turned out 359,489 of them. Ford built another 227,000 under license.

The Jeep's reputation as mainly a

Opposite page: One 1942 Willys ad promoted the Jeep's ruggedness with the line "Like a Bat Out of Hell." Shown is a typical example from that year. Stark but functional describes both the basic design and its execution (owner: Mike Scholer). This page: A close-up look at the 1945 example. Novel swing-up headlamps aided night repairs on the four-cylinder "Go-Devil" engine. Many special items were developed and fitted as needed, such as the dash-mount rifle cover (upper left) (owner: Dale P. Aylward).

Willys creation is owed to company president Joseph Frazer. Though he had little to do with its design, he had plenty to do with its publicity, and helped the public forget that Ford was making them too. He even claimed to have coined the name—from G.P., "general purpose," the Army's original description—though some insist it was borrowed from the "Popeye" cartoon character.

In all, wartime Jeep production was over 585,000 units. Military production would continue after the war, of course, but Willys wasted no time putting the concept in "civvies." First came a modified version dubbed CJ, for "civilian Jeep," followed in 1946 by an all-steel station wagon loosely based on the original design.

The military Jeeps were tough, versatile, and highly adaptable. But most of all they were loved. Bill Mauldin's famous 1944 cartoon said it best, without words. A grizzled, sad-faced sergeant, eyes covered with one hand, is aiming a pistol at his Jeep to put it out of its misery. Every military man and woman understood. But some may have wondered whether any Jeep was ever beyond repair. Surely it could be mended just one more time.

WILLYS JEEPSTER 1949

Open body styles with snap-in side curtains for weather protection—the roadster, phaeton, and touring car—disappeared in the Thirties as convenience-minded buyers flocked to styles with roll-up windows. But the phaeton made a surprise return in the late Forties. Of course, we're talking about Willys's jaunty Jeepster.

The military Jeep had given Willys-Overland a new lease on life during World War II and would prove to be its postwar salvation. Long a builder of large, often costly cars, the once-moribund Toledo firm had found salvation in the Depression with pioneering four-cylinder compacts that were cheap to buy and operate but somewhat oddly styled and not very profitable. Joseph W. Frazer, who took over from Ward Canaday as company president in 1939, came up with a much improved version, the patriotically named Americar of 1941-42. It was only a fair success, though, and Frazer's wartime successor, Charles E. Sorenson, decided W-O should abandon passenger cars after the war in favor of specialty products that could carve out their own market niche. The

Car or utility vehicle? The compact 2WD Jeepster was a bit of both. Snap-in side curtains augmented the weather protection of the manually folding top, which had a surprisingly simple metal framework. Small gauge cluster was mounted low on the dash center (owner: Al DeFabrizio).

Jeep concept offered intriguing possibilities, and designer Brooks Stevens quickly came up with two logical spin-offs: a station wagon (with a pickup truck derivative) and a four-seat convertible. The former, dubbed "Station Sedan," bowed for 1946. Technically, it was the industry's first all-steel wagon, though it's usually considered a truck, not a car. Stevens suggested the ragtop was technically a phaeton because it lacked a rumble seat and retractable door glass. He also suggested its name, a clever combination of "Jeep" and "roadster."

Willys didn't begin building the Jeepster until April 1948, rather late for that model year. Even so, it moved a respectable 10,326 of them despite the short selling season and a rather steep $1765 initial list price. Ads described it as "distinctly personal," a "dashing sports car" with "continental styling." And indeed, Stevens managed to relate the Jeepster to its legendary military cousin while giving it a cheery, devil-may-care demeanor. With its boxy lines, stubby 104-inch wheelbase, and compact 174-inch overall length, the Jeepster looked tall yet stood only 62 inches high with the top up. Contributing to this effect was a generous eight-inch ground clearance, which implied off-road capability, though the Jeepster had only two-wheel drive instead of 4WD as on its Army predecessor. Unlike the Jeep, however, the new phaeton had doors and rear fenders.

Weighing in at 2468 pounds, the Jeepster was built on a box-section X-member chassis with Willys's odd "Planadyne" front suspension. This consisted of single independent upper A-arms and a transverse leaf spring, and combined with a simple leaf-sprung live rear axle for decent handling and cornering. However, the ride was *rough*, a clear sign of the Jeepster's origins. Initially, power was supplied by the 134.2-cubic-inch L-head four familiar from the Jeep and the last Americars, still rated at 63 horsepower. For 1949, Willys offered a 72-bhp, 148.5-cid six, the smallest in the industry, for about $35 extra. Standard equipment included overdrive, chromed step plates for rear seaters, a 60/40 split front seat, and a simple rectangular instrument cluster.

Jeepster prices and production both fell appreciably for 1949. The four-cylinder version came down to $1495 and saw 2307 deliveries. The six-cylinder model dropped to $1530 but saw only 653 copies. For 1950, the vertical-bar grille was replaced by a V-shaped horizontal affair, overdrive became an $80 option and, at mid-season, Barney Roos's clever ohv F-head conversion of the old four arrived. The Jeepster continued in this form through 1951, when it was replaced as Willys's "car" by the new Aero line. Final year production, including re-serialed '50s sold as '51s, totalled 4066 Fours and 1779 Sixes.

The Jeepster would return in the early Sixties (via Kaiser-Jeep) as the Commando, but the early postwar models are the ones that attract the most interest today. They were a winsome reminder of the past at a time of design transition, an idea often copied since but seldom bettered.

Above: The Jeepster looked most like its military cousin from the front, but sported chrome trim for a dressier appearance. Right: Rugged but puny 63-bhp four was a prewar holdover. A six was offered beginning with the 1949 models (owner: Al DeFabrizio).